THE GREATEST STORIES NEVER TOLD: COVERT OPS

THE GREATEST STORIES NEVER TOLD: COVERT OPS

LAURENCE J. YADON

LYONS
PRESS

Guilford, Connecticut

An imprint of The Rowman & Littlefield Publishing Group, Inc.
4501 Forbes Blvd., Ste. 200
Lanham, MD 20706
www.rowman.com

Distributed by NATIONAL BOOK NETWORK

Library of Congress Control Number: 2020950300

ISBN 978-1-4930-4818-2 (paper : alk. paper)
ISBN 978-1-4930-4819-9 (electronic)

♾™ The paper used in this publication meets the minimum requirements of American National Standard for Information Sciences—Permanence of Paper for Printed Library Materials, ANSI/NISO Z39.48-1992.

For my parents, Helen Edmonds Yadon and Laurence J. Yadon

Contents

Introduction

The very word secrecy is repugnant in a free and open society; and we are as a people inherently and historically opposed to secret societies, to secret oaths and to secret proceedings . . . Our way of life is under attack. Those who make themselves our enemy are advancing around the globe . . . no war ever posed a greater threat to our security. If you are awaiting a finding of "clear and present danger," then I can only say that the danger has never been more clear and its presence has never been more imminent . . . For we are opposed around the world by a monolithic and ruthless conspiracy that relies primarily on covert means for expanding its sphere of influence—on infiltration instead of invasion, on subversion instead of elections, on intimidation instead of free choice, on guerrillas by night instead of armies by day. It is a system which has conscripted vast human and material resources into the building of a tightly knit, highly efficient machine that combines military, diplomatic, intelligence, economic, scientific and political operations. Its preparations are concealed, not published. Its mistakes are buried, not headlined. Its dissenters are silenced, not praised. No expenditure is questioned, no rumor is printed, no secret is revealed.

—PRESIDENT JOHN F. KENNEDY

THE BOOK THAT YOU NOW HOLD IS THE SIXTH IN A SERIES LAUNCHED WITH my friend, coauthor, and military historian, the late Robert Barr Smith, in 2016. These pages take the reader on little-known, yet unforgettable adventures with mostly American soldiers, marines, and sailors who conducted secret military missions, now called covert operations, from the American Revolution to the present.

A covert operation is a military, intelligence, or law-enforcement mission planned and executed to conceal the identity of the sponsor. Usually, but not always, covert operations are carried out clandestinely outside official channels. Clandestine operations, on the other hand, are ideally carried out under circumstances in which hardly anyone, particularly the general public, is aware that it has been conducted. Covert operations have become a more significant part of American foreign policy since World War II and have accelerated in the post-9/11 era.

Late twentieth-century and early twenty-first-century operations in the post-9/11 era have hardly been neglected in these pages. In fact chapter 12 focuses on the late-October 2019 death of Abu Bakr al-Baghdadi, who blew up himself and two of his children in an explosion as American covert operations specialists surrounded him. The Baghdadi mission concluded so close to the submission deadline for this work that the only reliable written sources available were newspaper and periodical articles written by well-respected, objective journalists reporting for top-shelf sources such as the *London Times, Wall Street Journal,* and *New York Times.*

When multiple sources for this book were available, they were carefully reviewed and compared, with a distinct preference for carefully vetted memoirs favorably reviewed by knowledgeable, experienced, widely recognized experts. Sources for the American Revolution, World War II, and other conflicts prior to 9/11 include eyewitness accounts and histories compiled in many cases by military historians.

Another preference was, whenever possible, to present these stories in the voices of those who experienced them. In some cases quoted materials have been modernized where appropriate and modified slightly to facilitate sentence transitions and enhance readability. Likewise, military ranks and abbreviations have been conformed to the maximum extent possible. The names of military operations in which several nations or armed services participated have been standardized. Lengthy names have been abbreviated.

This book puts the reader in the middle of covert operations conducted during the American Revolution, the War of 1812, the Civil War, World War II, Vietnam, and post-9/11 conflicts.

And it begins with covert operations conducted during the American Revolution by the least likely of characters—that famous bookworm, inventor, and diplomat, Benjamin Franklin.

CHAPTER 1

The Black Prince

ALL WAS QUIET THAT NIGHT AT POOLBEG, A PENINSULA JUTTING INTO THE ocean near Dublin, which sheltered at least two hundred ships, most notably the *Friendship*, a smuggling cutter whose crew had been arrested at sea on February 19, 1779. Their cargo of now-confiscated French brandy and Dutch tea was bound for His Majesty's customhouse, come morning. Just to be sure that the *Friendship* stayed in British hands, some nine revenue service officers now rested on board, in a stillness that would not last.

Everything seemed secure enough to the British guards a few days later. After all, last summer, in 1778, Dublin and its port had been strengthened in response to threats from the French king, who vowed hostility toward Britain. There had been other threats. On Friday, November 13, 1778, John Paul Jones, founder of the American Navy, led the only American invasion of England ever conducted, burning the coastal port Whitehaven to the ground.

Now, in 1779, the Poolbeg Lighthouse at Dublin, built just eleven years earlier, was protected by so many floating batteries that only two men were posted fore and aft on *Friendship* that night, as nine or so other revenue men snored their way through the night.

Apparently neither guard had any idea that they were in any danger. The *Friendship* crew was lodged in the Black Dog, a prison in Dublin. That made things all the easier for the two boats full of smugglers that pulled up on either side of *Friendship*. William Bell Clark observed in *Benjamin Franklin's Privateers: A Naval Epic of the American Revolution*, a principal source for this chapter, that the guards noticed the danger only when it was too late to sound the alarm. Clark recounts, just as the smugglers, heavily armed were over the bulwarks and upon them. No time then to give the alarm or even snap a pistol. Shouts for their slumbering comrades were stifled by blows from pistol stocks, stunning both men. The petty officer in the stern cabin, befuddled by sleep, was overpowered, bound, and gagged. The bewildered ones below were called up on the companionway ladder, one at a time, relieved of their weapons and neatly trussed. Not a shot had been fired; not a voice rose to a pitch which might have alarmed the shore. But the cutter still lay within hailing distance of the customhouse and darkness had begun to lift.

Most of the eighteen men had just broken out of the Black Dog, along with others who had helped them escape. Names such as Dowlin, Connor, Mulvaney, and Rooney tell us that most of these smugglers were Irish, with a few others from Wales and Cornwall. Their twenty-five-year-old leader, the owner of *Friendship* was Luke Ryan, who had been ashore when *Friendship* had been seized. Ryan swung into action immediately, developing the escape plan and recruiting help some twenty miles north of Dublin at Rush, then Smuggler Central in Ireland.

Ryan claimed later that he was a Frenchman by birth, the son of a captain in Dillon's Irish regiment in service of France. In fact he was the only child of Michael and Mary Ryan of Kenmure, near Dublin, where Luke was born. Instead of following his father into farming, young Luke served an apprenticeship with a ship carpenter before becoming a professional smuggler. In this occupation "he demonstrated a mind keen in outwitting the law, a character for audacity in landing cargo, a reputation for courage and a natural capacity as a leader. With intuitive knowledge of seamanship, he had commanded a smuggling wherry [boat] of his own before reaching his majority." He became anathema to His Majesty's revenue officers from Belfast to Dover.

Friendship sailed for Cardigan Bay, ninety-six miles to the Southeast, where crew members unloaded the brandy, the tea, and a disgruntled crew member named Bowen who was convicted of piracy about a year later. And with that, Ryan made the most important pitch of his life. They should become Americans.

His reasoning was simple: "No longer would the British regard them as smugglers who, if captured, would be given short prison terms and whose vessel and cargo might be confiscated. Retaking the cutter from the royal collector of the revenue, along with wounding several of his officers was a crime punishable by death." Only a few hours ago, they had become pirates so far as the British government—and most Englishmen—were concerned. Should the British capture them, they would be hanged.

Instead, Ryan argued, they should sail for Dunkirk, find a merchant to finance *Friendship* as a privateer, and get a commission from the Americans. His brash legal reasoning was that "as American subjects they might be immune, if captured, from criminal prosecution and be regarded as prisoners of war." To a man, the crew said yes.

The term *privateer*, sometimes applied to a ship like *Friendship*, also described a ship captain or crew members operating essentially as pirates with government protection. More precisely, a privateer was any individual granted license by a government to attack shipping belonging to an enemy government, usually during a war. Privateers were like private contractors. They received a Letter of Marque from their nation's Admiralty, which granted them permission to raid enemy ships and keep a percentage of the spoils—as long as they paid a cut of that bounty back to the government. The bearer of the Letter of Marque would then go about hiring his or her own crew and ship at their own expense. A privateer operated legally, so long as he had a Letter of Marque.

And so, *Friendship* sailed through St. George's Channel, past Land's End, and into the English Channel, fighting a storm so strong that the boom was lost. Undeterred, Ryan followed the coast past Calais into Dunkirk some two weeks later in early April 1779.

Ryan had no way of knowing that the already-famous American patriot Benjamin Franklin of all people was looking for just the kind of crew and ship that Ryan had to offer. Franklin, then serving as one of three American commissioners to the French court at Versailles, had run out of British prisoners to exchange for Americans being held in English prisons. Mid-March found Franklin recovering from gout in Passy, a tony suburb boasting numerous chateaux then about three miles outside Paris. William Bell Clark observed, "Almost nine months had elapsed since his persistency had won reluctant agreement from the Ministry in London to exchange American prisoners in England for British prisoners in France. Some 100 Americans currently held in the Mill prison in Plymouth would be sent to Nantes, France, with a similar number of British returned to England. After that a second load of Americans would arrive from Forton Prison at Portsmouth." The problem was that no shipload of Americans had arrived, leading Franklin to believe that he had been deceived. He also feared that some, if not all, of the prisoners had been enticed to obtain their freedom from prison by serving in the

British Army. He had specific intelligence reports indicating that the men in both prisons were visited from time to time by agents paid to tell the prisoners how bad they were being treated, even though the British were more than willing to trade them for English captives, thanks to Benjamin Franklin. The message was clear: Join the British Navy or be hanged as a traitor.

Beyond this, the British were taking far more "prizes" in European waters than the Americans were. Not only that, most American vessels that had ventured there had been captured by the British. Lightly armed American ships brimming with wheat and tobacco bound for France and other European countries were sitting ducks for the British Navy, as the captain of *Phoenix* out of Salem, Massachusetts, bound for Bourdeaux discovered the hard way.

After Franklin offered a change in terms to equalize the number of prisoners exchanged and was rebuffed, he considered commissioning privateers as a means of getting British prisoners to exchange for Americans. Franklin had a drawer full of commissions signed by John Hancock, president of the Continental Congress, before Hancock retired and returned to Massachusetts. Technically, these privateer commissions were no longer valid.

Franklin's first privateering venture quickly floundered when the sloop he commissioned was incompetently rebuilt for privateer service and had to be scrapped, manned though it was by Frenchmen, Americans, and even some Englishmen. Discouraged by this blunder, Franklin had declined to commission the burgomaster (mayor) of Dunkirk, who equipped a fourteen-gun brig to serve as a privateer.

Now, in April 1779, yet another privateering request sat in front of Franklin. This request was from Steven Marchant, a Boston shipmaster who had been in Passy three months earlier after escaping from England. Although Franklin supplied Marchant with passage funds for the return to America, instead of returning home Marchant went back to Dunkirk, where the mayor offered him command of his brig. Franklin wrote Marchant for an explanation of why he didn't simply ask the French for such a commission. Marchant never replied.

Good news arrived on April 8. A British ship arrived at Nantes with ninety-seven American prisoners. The bad news was that Franklin did not have enough British prisoners to exchange for the rest of the Americans.

A French noble with an interest in all things naval arrived in early May, with a possible albeit partial solution to the "prisoner gap." M. Sutton de Clonard had spotted a very fine cutter armed with sixteen guns in the Dunkirk harbor. He noted that Dunkirk was full of Irish smugglers, who, when combined with a few available Americans would make a good privateer crew. Clonard dropped Franklin a note just a few days later advising that their mutual acquaintance Steve Marchant would soon be dropping by Passy to request a privateering commission. Clonard urged Franklin to grant one.

No doubt Franklin remembered that Marchant had not responded to his inquiry about getting a French commission, but before Marchant arrived in Passy, somebody else arrived to vouch for him. Francis Jean Coffyn of Dunkirk had served as an agent for the American commissioners for several years, managing a small fund used for the relief of escaped American prisoners. Coffyn described Marchant as "an able but simple-minded seaman who had originally fallen into bad hands." John Torris and his brother Charles were Flemish men from Dunkirk whose ship was destined to become an American privateer.

Franklin apparently asked enough questions to discover that the 120-ton brig had already been outfitted, armed, and provisioned, sporting sixteen four-pound guns and some seventy men. Captain Marchant nominated one Jonathan Arnold to be his second in command.

According to William Bell Clark :

Doctor Franklin considered the matter for a day. Commissioning the privateer, as he knew from past experiences, would involve him in many troubles. On the other hand, encouraging such an armament was the only way he could hope to attain the exchange of more Americans in England. Should this cutter, rejected by him, go forth under a French commission, the prizes she would take would be the property of France; the British sailors she would bring in would be exchanged for Frenchmen. That would be of no service to his American countrymen in British prisons. He weighed the inconveniences and annoyances which might, and most likely would arise should he issue the commission against the satisfaction of freeing more men from captivity. His humanitarian interest tipped the scales in behalf of the prisoners.

In that sense, the decision was easy. He directed his seventeen-year-old grandson Temple Franklin to bring him a blank commission, blank bond, and a copy of the oath of allegiance. Franklin endorsed a commission signed by John Hancock dated in early October 1777 to read: "This commission is delivered by B. Franklin, Minister of the United States at the Court of France to Captain Marchant at Passy, May 19, 1779." Of course there were spaces for the shipowners' names to be filled in later to supplement the captain's signature, not to mention a companion bond.

Franklin predated the commission for completion when it reached Coffyn at Dunkirk. His written instructions directed Marchant to bring in as many British prisoners as possible "to relieve our countrymen from their captivity in England."

And so the smuggling cutter *Friendship* became the American privateer *Black Prince*. Luke Ryan himself renamed her that for reasons that remain unclear but possibly relate to her "sleek lines, black sides and almost legendary reputation as one of the swiftest vessels that ever had run a smuggling cargo." Ryan had offered the Torris brothers a half interest in the cutter, in exchange for the funds necessary to outfit and provision her for a three-month cruise, along with wages for the largely Irish crew. Ryan insisted on an American rather than a French commission. The reason was simple: The Irish crew could not pass for Frenchmen if captured by the British because they only spoke English. This was important because privateers, unlike pirates doing the same work, were not considered common criminals.

Coffyn and Clonard likely did not know that the Irish smuggler Luke Ryan was behind the arrangement proposed to Benjamin Franklin, with Marchant as nominal commander, but it was time to find a crew. Some thirty-six Englishmen and Irishmen with smuggling resumes from Rush, comprising about half of the crew needed, had come to Dunkirk with Ryan. The rest were recruited on the spot. Modifying *Black Prince* to carry a fighting crew would not be so easy. Major modifications would be required to make her a sixty-five-foot fighting ship with a beam of some twenty feet that could carry the necessary fighting crew. "The hold, which had boasted so many valuable cargoes, was now planked over from the forward gallery to the after platform, providing a berth deck with little headroom, but sufficient in length and breadth to sling fifty or more hammocks." Arming *Black Prince* was another matter. Although still painted black, additional gun ports and swivel stocks next to the bulwarks were added. Her armament now boasted sixteen 4-pounder cannons and thirty swivels.

Black Prince sailed westward toward England from Dunkirk on June 12, 1779 with as many of her guns hidden as possible, fully intending to board British packets running between Dover and Calais. The first few days were a bust. They first seized a Portuguese brig carrying British goods and a Danish ship bound for Dublin with a load of lumber, but the French Admiralty judge in Calais ruled that neither was a legitimate war prize and released them.

Sunday, June 13 brought better luck on the twenty-mile sea route between Calais and Dover.

Toward midnight they fell in with a large ship beating up channel. They took her to be an British merchantman en route to London and gave chase. She was easy to overhaul, came to [halted] promptly on their hail, and proved another disappointment, a Dutch West Indiaman bound to Amsterdam. She mounted enough heavy guns to have blown the *Black Prince* out of the water had she been an enemy. Monday, they sailed southwestward close in with the English coast boarding several prospective prizes only to find them neutral Dutch and Swedish ships. One vessel, appearing to be British, sheared off at the sight of them and ran for shore. They were close enough to identify her as a ten-gun cutter but could not come within gunshot.

Dawn Tuesday, June 15 brought another day of frustration. Black Prince chased six vessels into a small bay only to be rewarded with cannon fire from a British fort. Yet,

> *the day's excitement had just begun. Running out of the bay, they spotted another small fleet coming down around Beachy Head, coasters under strong convoy. Five of His Majesty's cutters could be seen in close attendance, and one of these detached herself to investigate. Marchant stood not upon the order of his going but clapped on all sail and fled westward, the enemy cutters on his heels. The Black Prince out sailed her pursuer until she lost her topmost irons forcing down her topsail. That changed the picture. The British vessel gained rapidly. Marchant plied his stern chases for half an hour to no avail. The enemy came abreast, so close that her captain, before pouring in a broadside, called out something which was heard but not understood. No damage was done. The Black Prince's 4 pounders answered with far more effective fire. Her Irish seamen, in the space of an hour, gave the cutter four guns to one and heard the British "cry most dreadfully." After five or six broadsides, their opponent sheared off.*

Later Marchant bragged that they probably killed or wounded a number of the British. That didn't stop him from chasing a cutter all the way back to the British fleet. Only when a frigate off in the distance off her starboard did *Black Prince* make for the sea, standing westward down the channel.

Luke Ryan knew from his smuggling experience that better prospects might be available west of Lizard Point, Cornwall, then and now nicknamed "the Lizard." Ryan knew the waters they were approaching between the Isle of Wight and Cape La Hague were likely filled with British cruisers. A frigate spotted on Wednesday morning only confirmed his concerns. "They spied her just after speaking with a Spanish merchantman who informed them that the fleet of Spain had sailed from Ferrol; a bit of intelligence of no practical use."

On Thursday, June 18 they spotted the British Grand Fleet about ten miles away, fortunately too far distant to be of danger to *Black Prince*. Friday was no more productive, but Saturday at twilight near Land's End their luck changed. First, they boarded a brig named *Blessing*. Within an hour, they boarded *Liberty*, and added the sloop *Sally* to the take about midnight, bagging a cargo of coal.

Sunday brought the brig *Hampton* "loaded with coal and earthenware and bound from Liverpool for London." The Irishmen seized *Hampton* at two o'clock in the morning. The sloop *Elizabeth*, carrying coal, oats, and butter fell into privateer hands an hour later, and this was just the beginning. Dawn brought *Three Sisters*, a smallish brig, followed two hours later by their seventh prize, *Orange Tree*, loaded with English peas bound for Cork.

Now *Black Prince*'s crew faced a problem. "About thirty-five Englishmen had been removed from the prizes and the hold would not contain them all. Some mingled above deck with the crew." Because this would be a real problem if a British warship came over the horizon, Ryan suggested that the privateers ransom *Three Sisters*, which they considered of little value as a prize. Implausible as it might seem today, in those days, the captain of a properly documented privateer capturing a ship far from a friendly port had the option of requiring the captain of the captured ship to agree on behalf of the shipowner to pay a ransom later. The ransom took the form of a bond and was usually enforceable

Black Prince's captain valued *Three Sisters* at seventy-three pounds in the ransom bill Ryan prepared, directing that the ransom money be paid to the order of John Torris, Marchant in Dunkirk, or his order in London. One disadvantage: The twenty prisoners loaded onto *Three Sisters* could not be exchanged for Americans held in England.

Some of *Black Prince*'s crew members were then tasked to sail the remaining six prize ships into Morlaix, a French port on the northern shore of the Brittany peninsula. There the crew would ask a French Admiralty judge for decisions declaring *Blessing*, *Liberty*, *Sally*, *Hampton*, *Elizabeth*, *and Orange Tree* war prizes. At least that was the plan.

Just after the captured *Three Sisters* cast off, a brig hove into view. Crew members aboard the brig *Goodwill* later claimed being decoyed toward *Black Prince* by a British flag before she opened fire. Of course, the Americans denied the false flag claim. Be that as it may, they boarded the brig *Goodwill*, which had departed London for Waterford in Ireland with a cargo of port, iron, and dry goods. This brig became the eighth prize taken in twenty-four hours, and it was the richest in cargo.

That Sunday afternoon, *Black Prince* set sail for Morlaix with *Goodwill* in tow. "Then the inevitable [British] frigate appeared to leeward. In her company was a vessel quickly identified as the sloop *Elizabeth*. That boded ill for the rest of the prizes. Their course brought them closer to the frigate, which hoisted French colors. No one was deceived. They hauled their wind, the *Goodwill* still in tow, and stood [sailed] due eastward." The chase was on for the rest of the day and into the night. Their pursuer, the British frigate *Quebec*, flying a French flag, chased Black Prince for some six hours before giving up.

Flying an American flag for the first time, *Black Prince* sailed into Morlaix on Tuesday, June 22, ten days after leaving Dunkirk. "She saluted the fort and kept on up the river to town. The *Goodwill* had beaten her in by an hour. None of the other prizes appeared, although one was reported in a port seven leagues to the eastward. Marchant hoped it was true."

It wasn't. The British frigate *Quebec*, which had hounded the Americans into Morlaix, recaptured six prizes, including *Elizabeth*. "The twenty-one Irishman aboard the prize vessels had wound up in a prison on Guernsey into which the recaptured vessels had been carried."

Marchant now reported to Benjamin Franklin: "Six of our prizes were retaken by the English together with twenty of my men." He admitted that he had freed twenty Englishmen but had kept twenty-one English prisoners now lodged in the Morlaix jail waiting to be exchanged for Americans.

The loss of the six prizes and granting freedom to twenty British sailors disappointed Franklin, who wanted as many British prisoners as possible with whom to chip away at the number of Americans held in English prisons at Mill and Forton. Soon thereafter, a letter reached Franklin on July 3 urging him to arrange for the immediate exchange of the twenty-one captured *Black Prince* crew members. Franklin's response to Marchant criticized letting so many British prisoners sail to freedom on the ransomed *Three Sisters*. "You should if possible have brought in all your [British] prisoners except what were necessary to sail the ransomed vessel because they serve to relieve so many of our countrymen from their captivity in England." Franklin suggested that if the same circumstances were to reoccur, Marchant should insist that the British being freed sign promises to get an equal number of Americans held in England freed.

Mid-July found *Black Prince* moored in Morlaix with a crew of fifty-one on board. Marchant added twelve of the British prisoners to the crew, bringing the men on board, including Luke Ryan, a part owner rather than a crew member, to sixty-four. They sailed on Thursday, July 15, encountered no British frigates initially, but lost a man who drowned while boarding a neutral Dutch ship. Their luck took a better turn after they rounded Land's End. Two brigs and a sloop fell into their hands off Cape Cornell.

They were so close to the Cornish shore that the exploit was witnessed from the cape. One of the prizes was a collier from the Welsh coal mines, the brig Lucy . . . she was almost in sight of her destination when captured. Another was the sloop John, carrying a cargo of copper and oil from Basset's cove, otherwise known as Portreath, a few miles beyond St. Ives Bay. The third was the brig Ann, with beef and other provisions bound from Bideford in Devon to Plymouth.

Marchant wrote into the journal from which he later derived his reports for Franklin that he sank all three, when in fact he ransomed them. An uncertain number of crew members on these vessels signed "sea paroles" whereby the signer agreed to add his own name to the list of British prisoners freed by the Americans. Not everyone on the captured British vessels was required to sign them.

Saturday, July 17, along the coast of Cornwall, *Black Prince* encountered and boarded three more vessels. Marshall unconditionally freed a dozen men from these vessels but insisted that the master of *Rebecca* and his cabin boy sign sea paroles.

Sunday afternoon, July 18, brought the Spanish brig *San Joseph* bound from Cadiz to Dublin with an expensive cargo of wine, cochineal, and indigo. They discovered on boarding her that the brig was already in the possession of British privateers, but they put two crew members on board to sail her to France anyway, because under the rules of Admiralty, they were entitled to half the value of the cargo.

Franklin's privateers stopped a number of ships in the days that followed, notably including the highly valuable brig *Dublin Trader* carrying a large cargo of oil, copper, tin, and dry goods, which they intercepted the afternoon of Monday, July 19. This attracted significant attention in Britain, as described in *Benjamin Franklin's Privateers*.

A great outcry arose throughout Cornwall, Devon, Somersetshire and Wales as the ransomed vessels and paroled crews drifted into various ports. Consternation seized those exposed shores from Land's End clear around to Milford Haven. Mounting rumors, exaggerated reports, wild fears were reflected in the letters that sped toward London as the quills of men of substance scratched and splattered urgent pleas for naval aid.

The authorities first learned of her approximate whereabouts, recounted Clark on July 17, "when the brig *Ann*, ransomed the day before, came into Penzance. The privateer was called the *Black Prince*, said the *Ann's* skipper, but he knew her to be an Irish smuggling wherry [boat]." All too soon the local populations learned that *Black Prince* carried an American commission but a ship full of Irishmen. "Then with inaccuracy amazingly close to the truth, he pointed out that in the ransom bill, the captain called himself Stephen Marchant, 'but his real name is Luke Ryan.' And to think, wailed a Penzance letter writer, 'We have no ships of war or cruisers on the coast.'"

Word traveled fast, soon prompting appeals to justices of the peace in the Penzance region, not to mention the Secretary of the Admiralty, who British citizens begged for immediate assistance "this Coast being totally defenseless, there being not one King's Ship stationed between Bristol and the Lands' End, to our knowledge."

The panic in Penzance spread, where merchants imagined that the Irishmen aboard *Black Prince* allied themselves with a number of smugglers headquartered between Padstow and St. Ives at a place called Newquay. "We are all in vast alarm [sic] here, for two nights the soldiers have been under arms'" one merchant "told a friend in Falmouth who had influence with their Lordships of the Admiralty, and who added his voice with a plea for a force to be sent into the North Channel sufficient to protect it against these daring Pirates." Local imagination alone expanded the Irish crew to ninety men or more. One area merchant complained, "I have been in trade over fifty years and don't remember such an insult to this coast before." Soon the *Black Prince* armament was magnified, at least in rumor to include twenty 4-pounders and twenty-one swivels and an escort with twenty-four 6- and 9-pounders.

Efforts to chase down *Black Prince* now began in earnest. A sixteen-gun privateer lying in Bristol Harbor put out to sea but sailed too late to catch her. British authorities considered moving some two hundred French and American prisoners held at Pembroke Castle in Wales elsewhere for fear that the *Black Prince* crew might liberate them. Complaints to the British secretary of the Admiralty asking for action against *Black Prince* went unanswered, as did the ransom bill for brigs *Goodwill* and *Three Sisters*.

John Torris, in the meantime, began planning for a second privateer, despite delays in the ransom payments and release of the twenty-one Irishmen held captive in Guernsey. The new privateer, to be called *Black Princess*, would be commanded by Edward Macatter. Torris recruited Francis Coffyn to seek help in these matters from Benjamin Franklin. Coffyn wrote Franklin explaining the Torris predicament, but Franklin didn't answer, at least not immediately.

The *Black Prince* set sail once again on Sunday, August 15, for the southwestern tip of England on a hunting trip northward past Milford Haven through St. George's Channel toward Ireland, with planned return, when the time came to Brest, on the coast of Brittany. The British whaling brig *Reward,* her hold full of whale oil, fell into Ryan's hands the next day, followed quickly by *Diligence,* another brig and the sloop *Friend's Adventure,* both of which were ransomed. The *Black Prince* captured and ransomed three coal ships, *Blossom, Resolution,* and the *Matthew & Sally,* a few hours before the *Betsey,* a sloop loaded with English pork came under their sway. The privateers battled a twenty-four gale before chasing the armed vessel *Spry* into the Waterford outer harbor, following some seven broadside battles between the two vessels. On the way back out to sea the privateers learned from that the *Spry* carried a two-hundred-man crew. While cruising near Hook Head, *Black Prince* bagged and ransomed the *Southam,* yet another collier (coal ship) for 2,125 pounds, $384,000 in 2019 dollars. Marchant reported all this to Benjamin Franklin from Brest and repaired a broken bowsprit, the spar extending forward from the vessel prow. The score against the British thus far: twenty-nine vessels captured in two months eleven days.

Franklin now forced by circumstances to act as an ad hoc judge of the admiralty struggled maintaining current records of the vessels and prisoners for which he was now ultimately responsible. Information he received from time to time from Brest and Morlaix suggested that the privateers might be able to scrap together seventy prisoners for the second exchange which he planned. He knew by now that, "Prisoners had a disconcerting habit of disappearing, either by death or escape or signing up with their captors to avoid the miseries of a French jail." In fact, eighteen of the thirty-two prisoners taken during the first two *Black Prince* cruises now served on her.

In August 1779, Franklin needed at least one hundred British prisoners to ransom Americans now held in English prisons. Early the next month Franklin realized that the *Black Prince* operation deserved more of his attention. Still struggling to learn arcane Admiralty Court rules and procedures sufficiently to achieve his objectives, Coffyn's request for a second privateer gave him pause. "Had the *Black Prince* brought in as many prisoners as he had hoped for, there would have been no question in his mind," said Franklin's biographer William Bell Clark. "He was proud of her exploits, but prizes and ransom by no means answered his aims. She could accomplish these results just as well under the French flag. The sole advantage to him of an American commission was prisoners. Unless he could be assured that more of them would be brought in, or more paroles taken at sea, he had no desire to become entangled in irritating disputes or judgments on prizes."

Franklin wrote Coffyn that he would get some legal advice and reply again later. He delayed responding to the Torris request for commissioning the *Black Princess* and read the French regulations on privateering which had been published the previous September. Franklin learned that he himself was responsible for writing legal judgments on prizes and ransoms to which the *Black Prince* investors were entitled. Franklin wrote the judgments the investors needed, but somehow his seventeen-year-old grandson Temple Franklin left the paperwork on *Goodwill* and *Three Sisters,* the two most valuable *Black Prince* prizes out of the mailing.

A few days earlier on September 4 the *Black Prince* sailed from Brest for one last ten-day cruise before the three-month crew enlistment expired. Before returning to Dunkirk, Marchant and Ryan hoped to capture more than a few more prizes, but a feud between them erupted the second day out. Ryan told Marchant "with no mincing of words that he had been allowed to consider himself the commander because by no other means could an American commission have been secured. There was no further need to carry on the masquerade. Dr. [Benjamin] Franklin would be advised that the captain was a mere cat's paw [front man] and a bungler, whose abilities were slight and who had been superseded during the voyage because he was incapable of controlling the crew and lacked initiative for aggressive cruising. Since the commission was in his name, he would be retained as nominal commander, signing the ship journal and necessary letters. But his power would end there; Ryan would issue orders hereafter."

Marchant had mixed feelings after this dressing down, but "was content to remain on board...only because there was so much at stake in the way of prize money." Nor was there any way of quitting the *Black Prince* had he wanted to do so. "He still had the semblance of authority due to his commission, without which the *Black Prince* would have been considered a pirate ship. A strong and intelligent man could have made effective use of this weapon to maintain his position, but Marchant was neither. He accepted the degraded situation and carried on the fiction, hoping to retain some dignity in the eyes of those unaware of his plight."

Everyone on board could see the change and no doubt discussed it even as the *Black Prince* rounded Land's End, passed the Scilly Isles, traversed St. George's Channel into the Irish Sea. One crew member journaled that on September 8 "Captain Ryan" fired a broadside into a Danish vessel and pillaged her. The next morning, a Thursday, the privateer ship intercepted *Hopewell,* carrying iron, tar and timber from Sweden just short of Dublin, her destination. Six crew members boarded the privateer and the rest were directed to sail the prize to Brest or Morlaix.

Within hours, while sailing northerly, *Black Prince* encountered the heavily armed revenue cutter *Townsend,* which Ryan initially misidentified as another privateer. Three *Black Prince* crew members, including First Lieutenant Alexander Weldin, were killed or mortally wounded in an exchange of broadsides before *Townsend* broke off the engagement.

After repairs and a sea burial for the three casualties, *Black Prince* chased a distant sail that came into view, only to discover that the ancient brig named *Peggy* wasn't even worth ransoming and burned it after removing the crew. After all these frustrations, Friday at last brought two prizes. The small sloop *Limont* yielded a cargo of pork, but there wasn't room in the hold for more British prisoners to exchange, because eighteen men from *Hopewell* and *Peggy* completely filled *Black Prince*'s hold.

In the twenty months that followed, *Black Prince, Black Princess, Fearnot,* and other vessels commanded by Luke Ryan captured or destroyed 116 British ships, captured some 161 British prisoners, and invaded numerous British towns and villages, forcing the British to engage hundreds of militiamen defending the coast while as many as forty British frigates chased Ryan's privateer ships.

That all came to an end for Ryan on Tuesday, April 17, 1781, just off the coast of Scotland, when the British 74-gun *Berwick* and an escort captured him while he was commanding the French frigate *Calonne*. Following a lengthy and highly public trial, Ryan was convicted of treason and condemned to death as a British subject. This, despite his claim at trial supported by documentation of dubious origin that he was born in Gravelines, a town in northern France. King George commuted his death sentence at the urging of Marie Antoinette, Queen of France.

Ryan died of blood poisoning in debtors' prison. He had been imprisoned for failure to pay a doctor who inoculated Ryan's three children against smallpox.

CHAPTER 2

The Patriot War

THE MEN OF THE US ARMED FORCES HAD THEIR HANDS FULL IN MARCH 1812, what with the threat of a looming war against the British only thirty years after the American Revolution. Still some Americans found time to fight the Spanish Empire for possession of East Florida—yes, East Florida—in a covert undeclared war, unknown to most Americans to this day. That covert war began on St. Patrick's Day with the seizure of Fernandina and Amelia Island. Problem was, the War of 1812, which began on June 1, wasn't going all that well. What then was the motivation for a covert action to take part of East Florida from the Spanish?

Historian John Cusick addressed this question in *The Other War of 1812: The Patriot and the American Invasion of Spanish East Florida*. His book served as a primary source for this chapter. In a real sense the dispute between the United States and Spain, Cusick wrote, "began in 1810 when American agents succeeded in destabilizing parts of Spanish West Florida and Texas." In that same year signs first arose that East Florida might be ripe for the picking. Five prominent inhabitants of Spanish East Florida, worried about the future of their province, conspired to rebel against king and Crown. The five potential rebels had diverse backgrounds.

An Irishman named Andrew Atkinson, once a merchant doing business in South Carolina and Georgia, had recently invested heavily in substantial East Florida commercial operations, along with the Spanish military commander at Fernandina, Lieutenant Justo Lopez, now an Atkinson partner in some Atkinson businesses. Area planters who joined the rebellion included

George Fleming, who had built his estate from the ground up along the St. Johns River, and John Houston McIntosh, whose ancestors and extended family were among the founders of Georgia. McIntosh was a seven-year resident of East Florida and owned several cotton plantations, not to mention laborers bound to slavery and all the cash these things could bring. The most noteworthy and interesting man among these rebels was Don Fernando de la Maza. Born near Santander, Spain, he interned in medicine at a Havana, Cuba military hospital and moved to East Florida, where he slowly began his ascent to fortune and influence.

The East Florida Five, diverse as they were in background, felt they had no alternative. Spain was in anarchy, thanks in large part to Napoleon Bonaparte, who had pushed Charles IV and Charles's son Ferdinand VII into giving up their kingly claims so that Bonaparte's brother could take their place. This prompted loyal Spaniards to take up arms against the interloper in 1808 with no success. Ferdinand became a French prisoner who could only watch as a "Regency" ineffectively battled the French in central and eastern Spain.

Word reached East Florida that Spanish colonials in Caracas, Mexico, Cuba, and even Puerto Rico were plotting to free themselves from the Spanish. In addition to that, American settlers in Spanish West Florida had taken up arms against Crown officials and were clamoring to join the United States. Under the pressure of these circumstances, the conspirators were willing to contemplate drastic action. They did not want East Florida to become a French colony under Napoleon. They did not want it to become a British colony either. And, if East Florida had to shake off its allegiance to Spain, they wanted to be the men in charge.

All too soon, in 1810, General George Mathews (not Matthews), an American citizen, veteran of the American Revolution, and former governor of Georgia, decided to join in the American effort to turn the East Florida colony into an independent American republic. After discussing all the details and possible options with the Americans there, he decided that this venture would easily succeed, even after their prospects were communicated to American congressmen, President James Madison, and several of his cabinet members.

Yet Mathews's report was not positive, because the five men promptly lost their nerve and abandoned the military initiative. More specifically, they changed their minds about their prospects should the American government invade or otherwise intervene in East Florida affairs, even as the seeming panic about Spain and the enthusiasm for some form of military action grad-ually diminished.

General Mathews disagreed and set his sights on seizing East Florida. He worked toward that goal for two years, culminating in the 1812 conflict that became known and the "Patriot War." Events elsewhere along the bor-ders between the US and Spanish colonies incited American frontiersmen to make something happen.

The United States had already absorbed the keystone of Spain's northern borderlands in the 1803 Louisiana Purchase. Now the Americans focused on what was then known as the Floridas. Spanish West Florida was a narrow area along the Gulf Coast that included Pensacola, Florida; Mobile, Ala-bama; and Baton Rouge, Louisiana. The long peninsula including the ancient capital at St. Augustine, the oldest continuously inhabited European settle-ment within the present borders of the continental United States, comprised Spanish East Florida. The problem for the Americans, in part, was access to water. Colonists and military forces in West Florida and East Florida were in a position to block or at least inhibit Americans in Kentucky, Georgia, and the Mississippi Territory from access to a number of critical waterways.

The ambitions of important American leaders coincided with these regional concerns. James Madison, who preferred avoiding military action if at all possible, had served as secretary of state to President Thomas Jefferson and long advocated acquiring these territories for the United States in much the same manner as that employed in the Louisiana Purchase. That said, after Madison himself became president, military action seemed the most feasible means of acquiring the Florida colonies. Madison did not hesitate to support American agents promoting rebellion against the Spanish in Baton Rouge (West Florida) and send in American troops to protect any American citizens living there.

Madison boldly told Spanish diplomats that their Empire would soon lose all of West Florida "between the Perdido and Mississippi Rivers." Madi-son insisted that the Spanish admit American sovereignty in that region, not to mention the Mobile and Pensacola districts, which could easily be expected to take up arms.

This successful "filibuster," as that term was used by the British to describe an invasion of Spanish American coasts, encouraged Madison to recruit General Mathews. The president commissioned Mathews to develop a strategy to sabotage Spanish rule in East Florida. Madison agreed to sup-port the Mathews plan, which called for efforts to persuade Spanish officials

residing at St. Augustine that the only practical alternative they had was surrendering East Florida to the Americans if possible and cooperating in an
active rebellion against Spain if necessary. Mathews soon notified Madison
in a series of letters that the political phase of this second Florida filibuster was unsuccessful. Hearing nothing from Madison, Mathews equipped
and personally financed a cluster of Georgia frontiersmen and a few Florida locals and dubbed them "the Patriots." Navy gunboats on the horizon
and the prospect of American Army support propelled the rebels into East
Florida on March 12, 1812, loudly yelling "Rise up" to anyone who would
listen. Formally declaring themselves "in revolt against Spain and—in less
than a week—forced the capitulation of Fernandina, then a bustling Spanish
entrepot [port] on the St. Marys [not St. Mary's] and Amelia Rivers."

American infantry forces, and even some American Marines, followed
them on the road toward St. Augustine even as makeshift emissaries made
their way into the interior wilderness of Florida. Much to the dismay of
the American forces, both the townsmen and the governor of St. Augustine
refused to surrender, despite being surrounded by the American forces.

These developments did not go unnoticed back in the United States, but
public opinion was divided. Citizens in neighboring Georgia were wildly
enthusiastic at the prospect of an East Florida invasion as a means of settling
numerous long-standing disputes with settlers there. Camden County, Georgia residents, in particular, longed for such an invasion as a means of settling
disputes concerning fugitive slaves and other controversies that had resulted
in shootings and duels. Elsewhere in Georgia, people spoke of the [Spanish]
Dons with contempt, resentful of a nationality that mustered black soldiers
into its provincial militias—a direct challenge to Southern fears about slave
uprisings. The Georgians also resented alliances that the Spanish had made
with the Creeks, Miccosukees [a tribe within the Seminoles] and the Semi-
noles. "Better late than never," quipped the editor of the *Savannah Republican*
when he learned that Fernandina had been captured.

Elsewhere, particularly in the North, enthusiasm like that emanating
from Georgia was scarce, to say the least. "We await some kind of explanation," wrote the *New York Exchange Post* editor. Worse yet, the US Congress
refused to provide any additional military support. Widely unfavorable public opinion outside Georgia prompted President Madison, somewhat in the
manner of the *Mission Impossible* television series, to "disavow his involvement and revoke assurances of aid."

The June 18, 1812 American declaration of war against England brought further complications in East Florida. Leading American military advisers, concerned with complications experienced in the Canada campaign, urged President Madison to establish a strong defensive position in Spanish East Florida, because at that time Spain and Britain were preoccupied with a war against Napoleon Bonaparte. Although the Spanish Regency had declared neutrality in the British dispute with the United States, neither then-incumbent secretary of state James Monroe nor former president Thomas Jefferson believed that Spain could be trusted to remain neutral in the months to come. In fact, American government officials feared that the Spanish might welcome British ships to numerous Spanish harbors.

Editorial writers expressed the fear that should British forces be introduced into the Florida territories, the United States might lose the Mississippi Territory.

Spanish governor Sebastián Kindelán y O'Regan was a son of Irish parents who settled in Spain. His father became a Spanish general. In response to a letter from Georgia governor David Byrdie Mitchell insisting that the Spanish disarm and dismiss the Black troops in their army, simply responded, "Retrace your steps, withdraw from our country and you will have nothing to fear from our . . . troops." O'Regan criticized the Americans for invading East Florida during a period of profound peace only to ruin the Spanish planters, starving the people in the Florida capital, claiming at the same time that "all is fair."

Benigo Garcia, writing on behalf of O'Regan, complained that East Floridians were exposed to "all the horrors of war" in an American effort led by the president himself to coerce Spanish authorities into ignoring their duties. Indeed, according to Garcia at least, the Spanish lacked the troops to expel American troops camped within the very shadow of St. Augustine, even as about a thousand head of Spanish cattle were driven off to the far reaches of Georgia. This loss, as well as ruined crops and the escape of African American slaves living in East Florida, were all attributed to American James Madison with a flourish of language suggesting that the otherwise enlightened American citizenry had somehow been lulled to sleep.

The Patriot rebellion grew into the Patriot War, even as hundreds if not thousands of Spaniards and Americans, Blacks, Native Americans, and Whites were caught right in the middle. The conflict began in 1812 and droned on for two years, prompting, among other things, conflicts with Native Americans. This was "war even to the knife," in other words an early form of total war that degenerated into scorched earth tactics, terror, and ambush.

The Americans invading East Florida expected a quick victory, but the Patriot War became a long-term stalemate. Because the US government was absorbed with the war against Britain, Patriot War soldiers "found themselves virtually abandoned in hostile territory, having no popular mandate either to proceed with or withdraw from their mission."

Tolerance for the Americans among the Spanish citizenry all around them, not to mention the Spanish soldiers and militia staring down at them from the walls of the fort at St. Augustine, rapidly diminished as the troops slaughtered tens if not hundreds of local cattle to sustain themselves.

Thus it was no surprise when the Spanish promoted Native American raids against small American forces using "guerrilla-style" ambushes that terrorized the Americans who survived them. This was a war of attrition, which spun off numerous personal vendettas between individuals and groups of individuals. Very few plantations between Cape Canaveral and the Georgia border were overlooked by "midnight ruffians from one side or the other looting or, worse yet, burning houses and barns to the ground." One observer complained to the *New York Evening Post* in a letter published on October 16, 1812, of plunder and even murder becoming almost routine.

Soon thereafter, Pedro Pons first caught sight of a strange-looking Patriot flag from his sloop sailing through a channel of Bells River some six miles west of Amelia Island. There it was, "fluttering on a pole in a field of knee-high corn shoots." The white flag bearing a human form carried the Latin inscription *Agilis populis, Lex Suprema,* meaning "the health of the people should be the supreme law." This was not the only Patriot War flag, as there were written accounts of at least three other competing flags bearing different mottoes. Not a single Patriot War flag has survived.

March 1812 found Fernandina on Amelia Island a loud bustling place full of sailors and street vendors offering their goods in loud voices, trying their best to overcome the nearby construction work on houses, warehouses, and even wharves. Some of this was caused by townspeople doing their best to conform with a new law requiring the community be laid out into streets and blocks. The town stood on a bluff some fifteen feet above the Amelia River, with an excellent view of nearby islands, waterways, planted cotton, cornstalks, and even orange groves.

Only the mouth of the St. Marys River into the Atlantic Ocean separated the northern tip of Amelia Island in Spanish East Florida from the southern tip of Cumberland Island in Georgia. Only a few miles away from Fernandina, American military officers at Point Peter quarreled among themselves in mid-March, even as reports of a potential attack began dribbling into Fernandina. Months later, in early March, George Clarke, a prominent Fernandina citizen told a friend that they had heard rumors about preparations for an American attack under way. More specific information arrived in Fernandina on Saturday, March 14. A pair of Spanish settlers along St. Marys River sent a message claiming that Americans were flooding in from Georgia, moving toward Fernandina. This was confirmed by one Don Felipe Solana late that evening, even as local Fernandina settlers dusted off their weapons and started night patrols.

Sunday, March 15 brought the American forces to Lowe's plantation six miles west of Fernandina, which they commandeered. The Americans offered terms to Spanish East Florida residents outside Fernandina, threatening land forfeiture against those reluctant to join the cause. The seventy-five-man American force doubled in size the next day. Spanish East Florida resident William McCullough said later that he joined reluctantly, even though he thought "the American government would be better than the Spanish."

While the Americans feasted off the Lowe's plantation cattle, chickens, and tame pigeons, John Houston McIntosh, one of the East Florida residents now leading the American forces, drafted a call for Fernandina itself to surrender. In the meantime, American gunboats went into action that Sunday. Two boats stationed at the mouth of the Amelia River began blocking passage to and from the Atlantic Ocean. One Spanish citizen, Justo Lopez, sent a polite inquiry to the Americans asking if the American government was behind this action and began coordinating a defense with the captains of the Fernandina militia. The nine Spanish regulars defending the tiny dilapidated fort in Fernandina had only a pair of 6-pound cannons partially buried in sand. The militia dug these weapons out of the dust, primed them with powder, and hoped for the best, even as local shop owners and citizens dragged in whatever shot, nails, and other scrap metal they could find.

The McIntosh ultimatum, read to several prominent Fernandina residents by candlelight that Sunday evening, notified them that "Wee [the American covert operation] have already secured all the country between the St. Johns and St. Marys, and, had it not been for an unexpected circumstance, we would have possession of St. Augustine and the fort tomorrow night." The note continued, warning the Fernandina citizenry that a pair of gun boats were approaching even as American forces increased "like a snowball," ensuring more than enough troops to conquer the entire Spanish province.

The author, presumably McIntosh, made no secret of his intention to put Amelia Island and everyone living there under a long siege, even as he invited them to rush into the embrace of American arms in this "glorious cause." McIntosh described the alternatives facing the Amelia Islanders in very explicit terms, telling them that in a worst-case scenario "no one" on the American side (and certainly not McIntosh) would answer for the consequences.

A tangible, dangerous threat lay hidden in this ornate language. McIntosh knew that two of the Spanish East Floridian stalwarts listening to this message, Justo Lopez and Fernando Arrendondo, had conferred with General Mathews in 1810; this was their last chance to join the American cause and save their estates.

Monday morning, March 16, brought Lopez an ugly surprise at the small, neglected Fernandina fortress. Somebody had sabotaged the 6-pound cannon, driving a long nail into the touchhole. The sergeant of the few regular troops in residence admitted that this was his work; he had misinterpreted orders to place nails near the gun *just in case* it had to be spiked. This left a single 6-pound cannon to defend Fernandina, even as small arms began to inexplicably disappear from the fort as the day progressed, likely the work of Patriot agents.

During a council of war that followed, the Fernandina elite, comprised largely of men with English, Scottish, or Irish heritage, calculated their defensive force to consist of about one hundred able-bodied men, half of whom were men of color. Soon two Patriot partisans delivered yet another demand, detailing how the surrender would be carried out. First, the town garrison would march out, surrender arms, and receive paroles. Second, Fernandina would be ceded to the United States with the understanding that British commerce could be continued for one year. Third, the Fernandina residents would keep the timber-cutting rights granted by the Spanish government. In exchange for these concessions, the Patriot forces would respect and protect all private property, provided that commissioners from Fernandina appeared immediately at Lowe's plantation to negotiate more specific terms for the surrender.

At ten o'clock in the morning, Fernandina residents were watchful yet optimistic, because the American Patriots had made a number of threats but didn't follow through on any of them, even as Spanish reinforcements arrived in ever-increasing numbers. Beyond this, British officers donated several barrels of gunpowder for the fifty or so muskets and several pistols were collected to complement the nine cannons that would defend the town as needed. Black militiamen were directed to leave the town square out of fear that their presence might provoke the Georgia men who soon might invade the town. Irate at this insult, several of the Black militiamen threw down their weapons and left the town square.

More testy discussions between the Patriot and Fernandina leadership cadres continued into the late hours of Monday, March 16. In the meantime, Major Jacint Laval of the American Army composed a letter to the secretary of war. "It is very important you should apprise the President of the danger the United States are in, of being involved in war with Spain, if the agent General Mathews is suffered to proceed." Laval complained of Mathews acting imprudently and encouraging other Americans, some sixty or seventy in number, to do the same, hoping to cover themselves with glory as patriots. "They take possession of places where there is nobody to oppose, declare it independent and send manifestos. General Mathews sees them—encourages them. How he will get out of it I know not; the whole must fall upon the government."

The next morning, five American Navy gunboats commanded by Commodore Hugh Campbell went into action in support of the Patriot force. Fifty men manned each gunboat, which carried 32-pound cannons that could be swiveled around to fire at any target, not to mention Long Tom cannons that could do equal damage on warships and thick-framed Fernandina houses. Worse still from the perspective of the residents: Those assigned to defend the town from behind cotton bales had little hope of surviving the point-blank artillery fire they might soon face.

Lieutenant Justo Lopez, the Spanish military commandant at Fernandina, "had between nine and sixteen pieces of small-caliber artillery" and some of this had been carried there from nearby ships. Lopez was outclassed by the gunboats, even though he could mount a significant barrage against the unarmed transport boats.

A meeting between Patriot leadership and some of the Fernandina elite at Lowe's plantation turned into an argument; the Fernandina representatives simply refused to discuss anything until General Mathews arrived. The Patriots agreed to wait for him for one hour but not a minute longer.

Mathews arrived just before the hour was up, claiming that he had orders from the US government to accept the surrender of East Florida from local authorities as if received from local Patriots. He claimed that "everything between Rose's Bluff and Lowe's plantation was already American territory." Beaming with generosity, he said now there were no outstanding orders from him to attack Amelia Island, but that the settlers should know that British forces were preparing to land Black troops from Jamaica in the near future.

Philip Yonge and George Atkinson, the de facto Fernandina emissaries, disputed the last Patriot point. They claimed that Lopez, the Spanish military commandant at Fernandina, might surrender to the US Navy, but he would never surrender to the Patriots. Mathews dismissed this comment as an irrelevant detail the Fernandina citizens must deal with themselves, because "the United States gunboats will not fire a gun, nor will they interfere with you, unless some British vessel should aid you, and in that case they have orders to fire upon you." Mathews hesitated a minute before saying, "And I am informed that you have been supplied with arms and ammunition by some [British] vessels that are now in port."

And with that, the quarrel began in earnest. Yonge and Atkinson insisted Fernandina had every right to ask for British assistance, with Mathews assuring them that if Fernandina did so he would fire upon the town. He realized now that the Fernandinans did not intend to surrender. Just as Yonge and Atkinson boarded their boat, a message from Mathews arrived.

It has been the voice of humanity and our desire to avoid the shedding of blood, which has delayed our march. I see, with regret, that your conduct has been equivocal and evasive, and therefore I inform you that the negotiation is at an end; and I charge you on pain of death to return to the island [Amelia] and inform the inhabitants that I will this day make my landing upon it; and I will not fire a single gun, or commit any disorder, if they do not fire upon me. But in the event they do, we will show no quarter, and we will proceed to confiscate the properties of all those who should do so . . . but if they surrender, I obligate myself, in the most solemn manner, to comply with my first proposals.

Five gunboats arrived in front of Fernandina, within pistol range of the plaza, by the time Yonge and Atkinson returned there, bringing a somber silence to many settlers who had not yet accepted the inevitability of American occupation. The sight of American gunboats on the horizon brought panic to both the militia and the local citizenry gathering on the plaza to assess the size and number of weapons that now confronted Fernandina. Their guns loaded with canister (small cannonballs) and grapeshot, the American sailors were charged and ready.

On board one of the boats, Commodore Campbell was sorting out what he considered contradictory orders. Earlier he ordered his commanders to come as close to the Fernandina battery as they could without beaching their vessels to be ready and able to help the Patriots accept a Spanish surrender.

Now, later in the day, he seemed to panic, sending up a series of signal flags and firing a signal gun for the apparent purposing of coaxing the boats hugging the Fernandina harbor back to the open waters to avoid firing upon a town that could not defend itself. His subordinate commanders were not all cooperative.

One Campbell subordinate displayed particular defiance, yelling to another boat commander, John Grayson, that Grayson could go back, but Winslow Foster, his gunboat, and crew were staying. Grayson hesitated, perhaps even considering the possibility of staying himself, before raising sail and cruising back toward Campbell with a second boat behind him. Despite a series of urgent signals from Campbell, commanding Winslow and the others to set sail, Winslow didn't budge. Having little choice as a practical matter, Campbell sent word to Winslow and the rest that they were not to communicate with, nor fire upon, Fernandina.

Just about then, soldiers hauled down the Spanish colors and a messenger rowed across to the gunboats "offering to surrender Fernandina to the US Navy, which refused the gesture." The soldiers raised the Spanish flag again. Sometime around two o'clock in the afternoon, Commodore Campbell ordered yet another series of gun-and-flag signals to his subordinate commanders mostly gathered at Lowe's plantation six miles west of Fernandina. Despite Campbell's orders, a number of these men clambered aboard seven or more flatboats in full view of several Fernandina residents watching them with spyglasses. Pushed along by a strong ebb tide, each boat, occupied by some thirty men or more, pushed toward the town, splashing about as if they were giant water bugs, according to some observers in Fernandina.

All of this froze Justo Lopez, the Spanish military commandant in place on his front porch, where he could do little but simply watch. After all, he commanded only some 100 men at the very most, these few being gathered in a place that was hardly defensible in any circumstance, much less his present position facing Patriot ground troops of some 250 men or more supported by Americans, some seamen sporting artillery. Lopez was conflicted, to say the very least. One thing was clear: He didn't have the weapons or the forces to make an effective fight, even though some of his men urged him to order a fight in what was obviously a hopeless cause. In the end, Lopez realized that so far as the Spanish were concerned that day and, in that place, all was irretrievably lost.

He looked about the room for someone, anyone, to carry a white flag of truce out into the Amelia River. One George Clarke (no known relation to the Revolutionary War general) stepped up, took the flag, and rowed out to the Americans. "Upon coming up with them, he told them that he was prepared to surrender the city and take down the Spanish flag." Cheers rang out from the Patriots crowded about flatboats ready for the attack. Clarke signaled Lopez that the mission was accomplished, so Lopez struck the Spanish flag even as American Patriots now about a mile south of town waded ashore marched around a marsh and took formal possession of the town at about five o'clock.

In the manner of those times, there was a brief ceremony on the plaza. "With the Patriots and the town militia standing in ranks, Lopez stepped forward, tears in his eyes and unbuckled his sword and handed it" to a man named Ashley, who strapped it to his waist. During the sunset hours, American colors went up the flagpole as startled local citizens looked on, even as gunboats sailed as quickly as they could into the Amelia River, making the Patriots masters of all before them, without a single musket fired or saber bloodied in battle. The second-largest town in Spanish East Florida practically jumped into Patriot hands.

CHAPTER 3

Children of the Mist

JOHN SINGLETON MOSBY STARTED HIS MILITARY CAREER AS AN ENLISTED man like thousands of others, with no real prospects for promotion. Yet he became one of the most distinguished, famous, or, in the eyes of his enemies, infamous, military officers of the American Civil War—all because of his unmatched skill at covert operations.

His grandfather, James McLaurine of Powhatan County, Virginia, had served in the American Revolution. John Singleton Mosby was born in early December 1833 at the McLaurine home, but his father began farming near Charlottesville in Albemarle County, Virginia when John was a small child. His fondest memory of those earliest years centered on a schoolhouse on an adjoining farm that was reduced to nothing more than a bare chimney during the Civil War. When he turned ten, young John rode a horse into Charlottesville for instruction in Latin, Greek, and mathematics. Soon he could recite Tacitus in Latin, but he preferred the stories of Washington Irving, none of which was as important to him as hunting on Saturday mornings.

John enrolled at the thirty-year-old University of Virginia (UVA) at age seventeen. Some sources claim that he graduated with a degree in Greek, mathematics, and philosophy, but that is not so. During his third year, on March 30, 1853, Mosby experienced some serious difficulty, which a classmate recorded in his diary. "Yesterday was a day of some excitement," the classmate wrote. "A student named Mosby—a graceless scamp—took some affront at some remarks made about him by Turpin ... also a student." Mosby wrote Turpin, asking for an apology, but when no apology was forthcoming,

Mosby went looking for Turpin and found him outside of the Brock boardinghouse. Apparently Mosby surprised Turpin just after dinner, quickly pointing a pistol at Turpin's face. Turpin tried to push the pistol away before Mosby could dead aim, but he was too late; he deflected the shot just enough so that the pistol ball entered his face near the corner of his mouth instead of between the eyes. Turpin would live to see another day. Kevin H. Siepel wrote in his biography, *Rebel: The Life and Times of John Singleton Mosby*, a primary source for this chapter, that Turpin was a known bully who insulted some trivial arrangements Mosby made for a party at the Mosby household.

Mosby was tried in mid-May. Acquitted of malicious shooting but convicted of unlawful shooting, he was sentenced to one year in prison and a five hundred dollar fine, about fifteen thousand dollars in modern money. During his confinement, a number of UVA students, including some who served with him later during the Civil War, visited Mosby in the Albemarle County lockup.

Virginia governor Joseph Johnson turned down several early pleas for clemency, but finally yielded on December 21, about two weeks after Mosby's twentieth birthday.

While he waited in jail and hoped for the best, Mosby, impressed by the trial proceedings he had just experienced, asked William J. Robertson, the very prosecutor who got him convicted, for a copy of Blackstone's *Commentaries*, the definitive pre-Revolutionary source of common law that was most often applied by US courts at the time. Robertson was impressed enough to let Mosby borrow any legal book he wanted from the Robertson law library in Charlottesville. After his late December release, Mosby went there to study the law.

❧

According to *The Memoirs of Colonel John S. Mosby*, less than two years later, in October 1855, Mosby became the first lawyer to open an office in Bristol, Virginia. His first experience with military matters was a pure coincidence. While in the courthouse at nearby Abingdon, Virginia in mid-1860, Mosby encountered his UVA classmate William Blackford, who just then was in the process of raising a company of cavalrymen. Strictly as a favor, Mosby allowed Blackford to include his name on the enrollment list, but he didn't even bother to attend the first muster. That November he told a Bristol newspaper editor which side of the coming conflict he would prefer to take—the

Union. Early in January 1861 he rode the sixteen miles from Bristol into Abingdon for the first drill.

After Abraham Lincoln became president, the Virginia Convention of 1861 convened in Richmond on February 13, 1861 to consider whether Virginia should secede from the Union. The first ballots all favored remaining in the Union. However, when President Lincoln issued a Proclamation on April 15 calling up state militias to suppress the rebellion, the Virginia Convention adopted an ordinance of secession. In a sense, the statewide vote on the fourth Thursday in May was only a formality.

Mosby started active duty as a private mustered in at Martha Washington College near Abingdon. May 30 found Mosby and the others mustered into the First Virginia Cavalry commanded by James Ewell Brown Stuart, better known as J.E.B. or "Jeb." Mosby's first assignment was a scouting mission to the vicinity of Martinsburg, about fifteen miles northeast of Harper's Ferry, Virginia. The First Virginia Cavalry participated in the July 21, 1861 Battle of Manassas, also called the First Battle of Bull Run. Picket duty on the Potomac and a posting to Fairfax Court House followed, but then on November 21 Mosby wrote his wife, Pauline Clarke Mosby, about a close call he had experienced.

"Colonel [Fitzhugh] Lee took about 80 men on a scout, hearing where a company of about the same number of Yankees was on picket, we went down and attacked," Lee remembered later. The Unionists hid in a pine thicket so dense that they should have been able to leverage their position tenfold—or so said Lee. He remembered the withering gunfire that poured into Rebel flanks, quickly separating Lee and Beattie Fount from the rest of his men. Lee recalled surprising two Union men in the deepest part of the thicket. He gave them a chance to surrender, but surrender was not in the cards. They responded to the chivalrous offer, but not in the manner Lee had expected. "One of the Yankees jumped behind a tree and was taking aim when I leveled my pistol at him but missed. He also fired, but missed Fount, though within a few feet of him. I then jumped down from my horse and as the fellow turned to me, I rested my carbine against a tree and shot him dead." Even though Fount missed the other Yankee, a South Carolina soldier stumbled into the fight and took him out. Minutes later, Lee went through the pockets of the man he killed and discovered a letter from the man's girlfriend, a woman named Clara.

February 12, 1862, a Wednesday, found Mosby riding away from Fairfax Court House in a carriage seated between two young ladies he would drop off near Frying Pan before returning the carriage to General (Jeb) Stuart's headquarters at Centreville. Then, he supposed, he would walk the four miles to his own camp nearby. Instead, Stuart insisted that he spend the night in headquarters, dining with Stuart and General Johnson, commander of the Department of Northern Virginia.

Later, Mosby wrote, "I never dreamed of Stuart's inviting me to spend the night at headquarters or that I should ever rise to intimacy with him." He remembered that he was as roughly dressed as any common soldier. "I obeyed and took my seat before a big blazing fire. Both of the generals were sitting there, but I felt so small in their presence that I looked straight into the fire and never dared to raise my head." He shared dinner that night and breakfast in the morning with Johnson and Stuart. "So here began my friendship with Stuart which lasted as long as he lived." That morning, back in his own camp, Mosby received word of his appointment to adjutant of his regiment, which became official on February 17. Mosby did not occupy the largely ceremonial adjutant position for long, nor did he help himself much with Colonel Fitzhugh Lee, nephew of the general, by calling a military bugle a horn.

One of Mosby's first important assignments for Jeb Stuart came to him at Bealeton Station twenty-seven miles northwest of Fredericksburg, Virginia. Mosby told his wife in a March 1862 letter that with the enemy fully in sight, he met with Stuart to discuss a reconnaissance request from General Joseph E. Johnston, who wanted to know whether George McClellan was really following Johnston with his entire army or merely pretending to do so for strategic advantage. Stuart, for reasons of his own, didn't directly order Mosby to do the reconnaissance but instead discussed how vital that information might be. Mosby, seizing this as an opportunity to show his worth, quickly volunteered, asking only for a guide who knew the territory. Once Johnston agreed, Mosby set out with a party of four. Their first challenge: flanking Johnston's army even as it moved toward the Rappahannock River. Mosby related in his letter home to Pauline Clark Mosby, his wife of five years, that "as the enemy moved south and we went north, my part was in its rear [behind McClellan] when the Union column reached the [river] and began shelling the Confederates who had just crossed."

Mosby rode his horse at a fast clip almost the entire night in order to report what he'd seen in person, but he ran into a serious problem as he crossed the river. Having stopped at a farmhouse for what remained of the night, Mosby rose at dawn, left his three companions sleeping, and started across the river himself, when a Confederate picket confronted him on the opposite bank, stopped him mid-channel, and threatened to shoot him. Mosby identified himself and tried to kid the guard, asking why he was so afraid of a single Yankee. Unamused, the Confederate guard signaled him across the rest of the river to the shore, his weapon leveled at Mosby the entire time. Mosby raced from there to find Stuart and report what he'd seen. Stuart soon recommended Adjutant Mosby for promotion.

Late April brought a setback: Fitzhugh Lee demoted Mosby to a private. Soon Stuart came to the rescue, assigning him temporary courier duty with assurances that an officer commission would soon arrive. In the meantime, small arms fire wounded General Johnston on the outskirts of Richmond on May 31 during the Battle of Seven Pines. Robert E. Lee promptly replaced him as commanding general of the army of Northern Virginia. Mosby later remembered an early morning conversation during the first week of June that arguably changed the trajectory of Stuart's career, not to mention his own.

Stuart had asked Mosby over breakfast to scout the Union position held by McClellan at Totopotomoy Creek, a tributary of the Pamunkey River. Off he went with three men, but he couldn't get through the lines to get the information Stuart wanted. Instead, he found a place to go behind Union lines and found something far more valuable than the general information he'd gone for. McClellan's lines near "the White House on the Pamunkey," then owned by Fitzhugh Lee, were fully exposed and vulnerable. This was the very place where George and Martha Washington had married.

Mosby concluded his scouting mission behind enemy lines on a very hot day and then returned at a double-quick pace to find Stuart sitting outside in a front yard. Military protocol then and now called for Mosby to give Stuart his report while standing at attention. Instead, Mosby collapsed onto the ground next to Stuart and gave his report as he recovered from exhaustion. Stuart listened to every word and then sent him to the adjutant's office nearby with orders to write down everything he had just reported. Stuart and a courier delivered Mosby's signed report to General Robert E. Lee himself. Soon, Stuart returned with orders to prepare the cavalry for an immediate mission.

Mosby recalled later that Lee's orders called for an attack on June 11, the next day. Stuart, in the meantime, moved out with his twelve hundred cavalrymen and two artillery pieces for Richmond and Ashland on the road beyond. When asked when he would be back, Stuart told the officer in charge that he might be gone forever.

Instead, Stuart's men, which included the 1st, 4th, and 9th Regiments of Virginia Cavalry, along with some men from the Jeff Davis Legion, drove north, edging the Union's right flank before driving eastward toward the peninsula. Outnumbered about one hundred to one though they were, they circled McClellan in a ride of some one hundred miles, raiding and burning supplies, not to mention destroying several ships along the James River shoreline.

One historian noted that this Confederate force rode through swamp water up to their saddles before undertaking a trip of twenty miles or so along the James in full view of the Federal army and numerous Federal ships and gunboats.

McClellan and the other Union officers viewed this large-scale horseback ride around the entire McClellan army within twelve miles or so of the very place where McClellan slept as a great insult. McLellan laughed and joked about it later, perhaps in an effort to soften the obvious blow to his reputation, but the effort did him little good. The Count of Paris, then serving as a staff officer for McClellan, described the incident as having caused a great deal of commotion in and among the Northern forces and serving as a portent of significant new and experimental Confederate cavalry maneuvers in the months and years to come.

Soon Mosby traveled to Richmond, bearing a letter from Stuart introducing Mosby to George W. Randolph, the secretary of war. Stuart informed Randolph in his handwritten letter that Mosby had, in the past few months, rendered the Confederacy "important and valuable" services at great danger to himself, entirely justifying a significant promotion. Stuart specifically recommended that Mosby be promoted to captain of a sharpshooter company. Lee also commended Mosby in General Order No. 74, a document publicizing Stuart's ride.

Mosby's promotion did not arrive for some time, but the Second New York, a cavalry unit, arrived at the Beaver Dam railroad depot about forty miles west of Richmond. The regimental historian later recounted that on July 19 "we captured a young Confederate, who gave his name as John S. Mosby. By his sprightly appearance and conversation, he attracted considerable attention. He . . . displays no small amount of Southern bravado in his dress and manner. His gray plush hat is surmounted by a waving plume which he tosses as he speaks, in real Prussian style."

Mosby himself recounted in his memoir that he was treated with the greatest courtesy. "General King," who was commanding Union forces there, "ordered my arms to be restored to me. In my haversack was a letter from General Stuart to General Jackson." Colonel J. Mansfield Davies offered Mosby Federal money for use in Washington, which Mosby refused. During the ten days of captivity that followed, Mosby carefully observed and mentally recorded everything he saw on his way to the Old Capitol Prison in Washington and back to the Aquia Creek Harbor on the Potomac for exchange. Mosby recorded what happened next in his memoir. He jumped off the boat onto the harbor landing early the next morning, located the Confederate officer in charge, told the officer that he had some important information for General Robert E. Lee, and rushed away to find him.

Sucking a lemon that he snagged somewhere along the way, Mosby set out toward Lee's headquarters, talked a South Carolinian into giving him a horse, and, long before he expected, walked into a house as the commanding general himself began studying a map.

Mosby maintained his composure while rattling off vital information to General Lee, informing him that Union General Burnside's force now reported directly to Union General Pope. After that, Mosby identified himself as being on Stuart's ride around McClellan, which undoubtedly brought a glimmer to Lee's eye. Lee expressed an interest in Mosby's opinions as to what the Union army might do next. In particular, Lee inquired about how, when, and where the Union attack against Richmond would be conducted. Mosby told him exactly what he thought, prompting General Lee to get a courier ready for a quick trip to General Jackson, then camped about eighty miles west of Richmond.

After several months' service beside General Stuart, Mosby's career in covert operations as a partisan began in early December 1862, after some service with the 1st Virginia Regiment near Spotsylvania Courthouse. He wrote his wife on December 9 that "during a scout [patrol] down to Manassas with nine men I stampeded two or three thousand Yankees. I see the Richmond papers give Colonel Rosser [of the 5th Virginia Cavalry] the credit of it. He had nothing to do with it and was not within twenty-five miles of there . . . General Lee sent me a message expressing his gratification at my success." Mosby asked his wife to send some of the works of Plutarch, Shakespeare, and Byron, among others. He went on to write Pauline that a few days earlier Stuart was so bored he decided to conduct a Christmas Day cavalry raid to Dumfries, Virginia in Prince William County, along the Union army line commanded by General Burnside, leading right to

Washington D.C. Mosby recalled chasing an entire Union cavalry regiment out of their own camp and then taking all of their personal effects and equipment. Then Stuart let Mosby conduct a smaller operation with six men, raiding Union outposts nearby, before putting fifteen men under his command for partisan warfare.

This was the beginning of what became an entire battalion, Mosby later recalled. Saturday, January 24, 1863 found Mosby crossing the Rappahannock River to begin a mission to "threaten and harass" the Union army along the border, in an area that Confederate General Joe Johnston had abandoned about a year before. The objective, as difficult and hopeless as it appeared to be from time to time, was to force the Union army to withdraw from the area, through periodic, deadly, and effective harassment.

Soon an admiring Confederate newspaper described Mosby for its readership. "His figure is slight, muscular, supple and vigorous; his eye is keen, penetrating and ever on the alert." Another description by a contemporary said, "He was thin, wiry and I should say about five feet nine or ten inches in height. A slight stoop in the back was not ungraceful. His chin was carried well forward; his lips were thin and wore a somewhat satirical smile; the eyes, under the brown felt hat were keen, sparkling and roved curiously from side to side." Another contemporary recalled some of Mosby's unusual characteristics: He didn't carry a sword, but did carry two pistols; had a low voice; and smiled a lot. Today he would be described as having an A-type personality. Mosby couldn't sit still for more than ten minutes. His eyes were unusual as well. "These flashed at times, in a way which might have induced the opinion that there was something in this man, if only it had the opportunity to come out." He was usually tan, was always beardless, and had a complete set of white teeth, which was unusual indeed in that place and time. One particularly apt compliment by a contemporary Confederate officer noted that "his activity of mind and body call it if you choose, restless, eternal love of movement, was something wonderful."

Mosby further described his early partisan days in his memoir. Southern men finding their way across enemy lines into his camp provided significant, useful information. Other sources at hand included simple observations of Union forces in and around Fairfax County, Virginia, assigned to defend approaches to the south of the nation's capital, while in winter camps circling from the upper to the lower Potomac.

The headquarters of Union Brigadier General Edwin Henry Stoughton in the town of Fairfax, then often called Fairfax Court House, became

Mosby's first target during this phase of his operations. Mosby directed his officers to select the weakest parts of the Union defensive perimeter for possible attack. Many of the Union sentries had become far too casual about these duties due to lack of action, thus providing opportunities for surprise attacks.

At first, Union leadership thought the attacks they began to suffer were conducted by local farmers-turned-guerrillas. Supposedly these men rendezvoused at sunset, conducted raids all night, and then returned to their own homes at dawn. That theory was dispelled when the Union men conducting raids on the homes of the suspected guerrillas often found the men in question asleep in their beds, only to discover when they returned to Union camps and outposts that Confederate guerrillas took advantage of their absence to conduct raids.

Mosby went on to describe his exploits against one of Stoughton's junior officers. Colonel Percy Wyndham, one of Mosby's early opponents, once served in Italy with Garibaldi, an Italian general and patriot. but now was in charge of outposts around Fairfax. He quickly became so frustrated with the successful Mosby raids that he wrote to Mosby and accused him of being a horse thief. Tickled by this claim, Mosby did not deny the charge but instead reminded Wyndham that every single Union horse Mosby now owned originally carried a fully armed Union man carrying a carbine, sword, or pistol—and in some instances all three. After attacking a cavalry regiment newly assigned to Wyndham, Mosby wrote to Wyndham saying that these Union men, carrying sabers and obsolete carbines, had not been worth capturing. He also notified Wyndham that each of Mosby's own men carried two Colt pistols that the US government had paid for.

Mosby wrote to his wife on Wednesday, February 4, 1863, describing a recent raid on a warm dark night. Although the ground was covered with snow, the snow was soft enough that Mosby decided to conduct an operation against a strong Union outpost near Fairfax, hoping to capture the outpost and all stationed there. This objective was all the more attractive due to the reports of many fine horses resting there. Several locals joined the operation. Earlier, Mosby recruited one Ben Hatton, a local merchant who sold goods in the Union camp in question, which was only about a mile from Hatton's house. Mosby and his men arrived at the Hatton house at midnight. A blazing fire at the Union picket post, where virtually all of the guards now slept, provided all the direction Mosby and his men needed. Hatton stayed behind with two Union soldiers Mosby described as "Jimmie, an Irishman" and "Coonskin," so known for the cap he always wore.

Mosby now described some of the confusion sometimes encountered in guerrilla operations. Hatton explained that some of the Union men attacked them, but he had no idea where the Federal prisoners, Jimmie the Irishman, or Coonskin were, much less how some of the Federal horses got there. Just about then, some of the Federals from the camp arrived and began to fire at Mosby and those under his command from a long distance, but made no effort to follow up with an attack. This left Mosby, Hatton, and the rest of the Confederates free to leave with the Federal horses and Federal prisoners.

He also described an action against a Major Gilmer that resulted in him being considered a hero when, in his opinion, the acclamation should have been for his horse.

Mosby and his men occupied Middleburg, but Major Gilmer was sent with some two hundred men to Loudoun, some seventeen miles to the northeast. According to Mosby, Gilmer "made his headquarters in the hotel where he learned that I slept. I had never been in the village except to pass through." Gilmer's orders were "to arrest every man that could be found and when his searching parties reported to him, they had a lot of old men whom they had pulled out of bed." Gilmer forced each old prisoner to ride double with one of his own troopers. In addition, some Black women with children doubled with Union men on horses. Mosby quipped that "when they started, the column looked more like a procession of Canterbury Pilgrims than cavalry."

Soon news came that Gilmer and his forces were at Middleburg. That prompted Mosby to gather some seventeen of his men for a gallop in that direction, with the hope that at least a few of the Federals could be captured. They learned in Middleburg that the Federals had just left, so they galloped on, with Mosby and some five men leading the way at a fast pace while the other twelve men conserved their energy at a slower pace. Mosby galloped into a little village called Aldie only to learn that Gilmer had just left. Thus, it was no surprise when, as Mosby and his small team ascended to the top of a hill, they surprised and captured two Union men who turned out to be rear guards for Gilmer. This prompted Mosby to send word back to his twelve rear guard Confederates that they should hurry up. Mosby spotted another two Federals, but this time he also could see the rest of Gilmer's force—an entire squadron of cavalry dismounted with their horses hitched to a fence. Outnumbered though he was, Mosby thundered toward the Gilmer force, because his own horse wouldn't stop. Lucky for him, the

Federals didn't realize that Mosby had only five men with him, and so they scattered in every direction.

In early March 1863, Mosby decided to capture General Stoughton and Colonel Wyndham. A captured New Yorker who turned Confederate "knew where their headquarters were." Mosby knew the place and its potential vulnerabilities to a night attack quite well. He recalled in his memoir that "the safety of the enterprise lay in its novelty; nothing of the kind had been done before."

The night of March 8 to 9 found Mosby and his men arriving at Fairfax Court House, then a village of four hundred souls or less, on a mission to capture Brigadier General Edwin H. Stoughton of the 2nd Vermont Brigade and his subordinate Colonel Percy Wyndham. Just after midnight they discovered that Wyndham had taken a train to Washington that very evening. Stoughton was not so lucky, as Mosby described in his Civil War memoir.

Once again, Mosby picked half a dozen men for a quick ride to an Episcopal rectory where the Union commanding general was staying. Mosby knocked on the front door prompting someone on the second floor of the house to open a window and ask who was there. Mosby identified himself as a messenger from the Fifth New York Cavalry who needed to see General Stoughton as soon as possible. A Union Lieutenant named Prentiss, clad only in a nightshirt opened the door and quickly realized there was nothing he could do about the Confederates standing in front of him. Seconds later Mosby and Prentiss were standing at the bedside of General Stoughton, who snored away, oblivious to the fact that he had just been captured.

Ever careful of the dangers operating behind Federal lines, and his present circumstances surrounded by several thousand Federals, Mosby decided "there was no time for ceremony, so I drew up the bedclothes, pulled up the general's shirt and gave him a spank on his bare back."

Later writers claimed that Mosby spanked Stoughton on his bottom like a child. Startled as he was at this rude awakening, Stoughton recognized his own staff officer but didn't see Mosby for a minute or two. And when he did, Stoughton asked Mosby what all this meant, only to be told he was a prisoner.

Mosby asked Stoughton if he'd ever heard of Mosby. Stoughton said yes. Mosby quickly identified himself and told Stoughton to get dressed. Stoughton asked to see Fitzhugh Lee, with whom Stoughton attended West Point. Two days later, on March 12, 1863, Mosby delivered Stoughton to Lee at Culpeper Court House. Stuart commissioned Mosby a captain on March 15. He became a major eleven days later, but more action came Mosby's way the very first morning of April, some seven miles from Dranesville, Virginia on the Leesburg Pike.

Mosby himself later reported what happened at a farm where his partisans camped the evening of March 31 for a night of peaceful rest. A guard who Mosby left on the Leesburg Pike to watch for the approach of enemy soldiers ran in and announced that the Union army was approaching. His announcement came only seconds before some of the soldiers were spotted a few hundred yards in the distance galloping toward the Virginians. Mosby's horses were eating in the barnyard nearby; some were not even saddled, they were all tied up.

Mosby continued: "Throwing open the gate, I ordered a countercharge, to which my men promptly responded. The Yankees never dreamed of our assuming the offensive, terrified at the yells of [Mosby's] men as they dashed on, broke and fled in every direction. We drove them in confusion seven or eight miles down the pike." Mosby's forces surprised the 1st Vermont Cavalry, consisting that day of some six companies, managing to kill a captain and a lieutenant and wounding another fifteen men so badly they couldn't be taken prisoner.

Sunday, May 3, 1863, brought yet another challenge. Union General Stahel later reported that "Mosby's band of guerrillas," together with part of a North Carolina regiment, came out of the woods and attacked some fifty men serving in the 1st Virginia Cavalry while as they were feeding horses, quickly forcing them into a nearby house. The Union men defended themselves, according to Stahel, as long as their ammunition lasted, even though Mosby's men gathered hay, brushwood, and timber around the house and set it afire, forcing the Union men to surrender, at least for the moment. Fortunately for the Unionists, part of the 5th Regiment, New York Cavalry, having observed the skirmish from some distance away, came to the rescue of the Unionist Virginians, charging and scattering Mosby's men. According to Stahel, all of Mosby's new prisoners and Union property were recovered. Stahel only regretted that his horses and men were tired out before this skirmish began. Had they been rested, Stahel speculated, not a single Mosby man would have escaped.

Mosby's later memoir did not specifically comment on this skirmish, but he recalled some of the complications confronting him at just about this time. In order to keep his relatively small force focused on guarding roads down which Union forces would soon be marching, Mosby had to "stimulate their enthusiasm" with material concrete results, such as capturing prisoners and seizing Yankee arms, ammunition, and supplies, because his men had little interest in "remote consequences," such as simply occupying territory to keep the Union army away.

Mosby requested a mountain howitzer on May 19, 1863. The light, bronze-barreled cannon manufactured in Richmond yet recently captured from the Yankees at Ball's Bluff arrived ten days later. Mosby gave his artillerymen a day of target practice before setting out with fifteen rounds of grape and canister and some forty men. Their mission: attack Hooker's forces gathered along a stretch of railroad between Manassas and Catlett's Station.

The very next day, General Stahel reported yet another fight with Mosby. This time he had little to brag about, because Mosby's guerrillas destroyed most of a Union train with the new artillery piece. Mosby's June 6 report to General Stuart tells the tale: "Last Saturday morning [May 30] I captured a train of twelve cars on the Virginia and Alexandria Railroad loaded with supplies." Just as he finished destroying the entire train in a huge fire, Mosby noticed that a strong Yankee force was approaching in front of him.

Mosby reported that a single cannon shell dropped right in the middle of their lines sent the entire Union force running away. This did not end Mosby's troubles, however, for he now learned that other Union forces were pursuing him from behind. His artillerymen momentarily stopped the pursuing Union men by firing yet another shot from the captured Yankee howitzer. Mosby reported that "in this way we skirmished for several miles, until seeing the approach of their overwhelming numbers and the impossibility of getting off the gun, I resolved to make them pay for it as dearly as possible."

Mosby directed his men to the best position he could find on a hill above the road that would soon be crowded with Union men eager for victory. And sooner than Mosby expected, the Yankees arrived, in four properly ordered columns, moving shoulder to shoulder down a narrow road toward Mosby and his men. "At eighty yards we opened on them with grape and followed this up with a charge of cavalry," Mosby said later, recalling the Yankee confusion. Having retreated down the road about half a mile, the Yankees charged twice only to be sent reeling backward.

Now out of howitzer ammunition, Mosby's men held on to the artillery piece as long as possible, forcing the Union men to pay a dear price for it. Mosby recalled later that his forty-eight-man force fought five Union regiments of cavalry that day, abandoning the bronze howitzer after fierce hand-to-hand combat in which former British officer Captain Bradford Smith Hoskins was killed. Four of Mosby's men were wounded that day.

This was hardly the last of Mosby's many guerrilla exploits during the Civil War. He led a raid across the Potomac River from Virginia into Seneca, Maryland on June 10, 1863, to chase part of the 6th Michigan Cavalry out of their own camp, which he then burned. In September 1864, six of his men were caught out of uniform in Front Royal, Virginia and executed. One of the men, William Thomas Overby, was offered clemency if he would reveal Mosby's whereabouts. He refused, saying, "My last moments are sweetened by the reflection that for every man you murder this day, Mosby will take a tenfold vengeance."

That didn't happen, but Mosby ordered seven Union prisoners executed that November. After three of the men were hanged, Mosby wrote General Philip Sheridan, commander of Union forces in the Shenandoah Valley, suggesting a mutual agreement that such practices stop. Sheridan agreed.

Mosby won his last battle of any significance at Kabletown, (West) Virginia with three times as many men as his adversary on November 18, 1864, but he was severely wounded in late December near Rector's Crossroad, Virginia. Gunfire through a window interrupted his dinner with a local family. Despite a mini ball in his stomach, Mosby managed to hide his coat bearing insignia of rank just before Major Douglas Frazar (not Frazer), commander of the 13th New York Cavalry, came through the front door, declared the wound mortal, and left.

Following Lee's April 9, 1865, surrender near Appomattox Court House, Mosby remained on the loose, ultimately surrendering on June 17, one of the last Confederate officers to do so. Mosby, then only thirty-one, practiced law, worked in the Federal government, and became the US consul at Hong Kong. A few hours before his death in Washington on May 30, 1916, of complications following throat surgery, Mosby reminded everyone present that it was Memorial Day.

During those last years, Mosby spent a substantial amount of time answering critics of his partisan tactics and practices. Before the war was even over, Brigadier General Thomas L. Rosser complained to General Robert E. Lee that partisan bands like the one commanded by Mosby had become a haven for men who sought to avoid battle. Rosser complained that his own cavalry troopers envied Mosby's men living at ease in private homes and keeping any Union supplies they could get their hands on. Mosby, using an expression Sir Walter Scott originated in his 1817 novel *Rob Roy*, responded to such complaints: "My men had no camps. If they had gone into camp, they would soon all have been captured." Instead, he recalled, "They would scatter for safety and gather at my call like Children of the Mist."

CHAPTER 4

Killing the Blond Beast

"Most days, he rode in the back seat of a Green Mercedes convertible to his headquarters in downtown Prague behind an armed escort. The convertible top was usually down, weather permitting. The weather seemed perfect that Wednesday on May 27, 1942 when Reinhard Heydrich took his last ride."

—AGENT PATERSON SOE: FROM OPERATION ANTHROPOID
TO FRANCE, THE MEMOIRS OF E.H. VAN MAURIK

ERNEST HENRY ("E.H.") VAN MAURIK GREW UP IN ENGLAND, THE SON of a Dutch father and English mother. His military service began in early September 1939 as a commissioned officer in the Wiltshire Regiment. A year later, while serving as an instructor at the Commando Training School at Lochailort, Scotland, he learned about the imminent arrival of twenty Czech soldiers who soon would be followed by twenty others. Despite the initial concerns he expressed in *Agent Paterson SOE*, his 1993 memoir, which serves as a principal source for this chapter, in a matter of weeks, he learned that even though the number of Commando students he now trained had doubled, they were already Czech army soldiers, most of whom had achieved a non-commissioned officer (NCO) rank and were commanded by a young Czech army officer with excellent command skills. Neither his Czech students nor Maurik himself knew at this point precisely which types of missions they ultimately would be sent on, yet this didn't matter at all, because what they really hoped for were assignments in direct action against the

Germans. During their training, they relished shooting rifles and practicing demolition against static targets they imagined to be the Hun, relishing a good time had by all.

Maurik assessed their discipline as excellent. Thankfully, the same Czech officer accompanied both the first and second group of Czech trainees. An English officer named Frank Keary used his excellent command of Czech, learned while teaching English before the war in Prague, to help them through training exercises in which they mastered combat skills.

Less than a year later, Maurik read about the assassination of German SS leader Reinhard Heydrich in Prague and soon discovered under an oath of secrecy that two of the Czechs he had trained had assassinated Heydrich with the assistance of several other former Czech students in a military action called Operation Anthriopoid.

The man they assassinated, Reinhard Tristan Eugen Heydrich, eventually nicknamed "the Blond Beast" by other Nazis, was hardly raised in a military environment. His father, a professional musician and opera singer, founded the Halle Conservatory of Music near Leipzig, Germany. His mother was an accomplished pianist who encouraged his early interest and lifelong passion for the violin. Despite these advantages, Heydrich was frequently bullied by older boys who ridiculed his Catholic faith, then unusual in a predominately Protestant town, and spread rumors that his background was really Jewish. He overcame these challenges, as well as frequent lashings at the hands of his mother to excel in academics and fencing, for which he received several awards.

Too young to serve in World War I, and perhaps as a means of fending off the Jewish ancestry rumors, as a sixteen-year-old in 1920 Heydrich joined the local chapter of Freikorps, a right-wing anti-Semitic organization primarily comprised of army veterans.

Influenced as well by the German Volk movement, which espoused the fictional superiority of blond-haired, blue-eyed Germans like himself, Heydrich sought and obtained a highly competitive appointment as a German navy cadet in 1922.

Now over six feet tall, skinny and angular, sporting a high falsetto voice and bleating laugh, his fellow cadets called Heydrich "Billy Goat" or "Moses Handel" to ridicule both his passion for classical music and supposed Jewish ancestry. Even as the ridicule turned to jealousy, Heydrich persevered, becoming a signals officer attached to naval intelligence with frequently expressed dreams of earning the stars of a naval admiral.

Those ambitions were excelled only by his pursuit of amorous adventures with young women, culminating in charges that he had sex with the young daughter of a shipyard director and refused to marry her. In one version of events, Heydrich was cashiered out of the German navy by Admiral Erich Raeder in 1931 at age twenty-seven for conduct unbecoming an officer. Help soon arrived with a new romantic interest, Lina von Osten, who recruited Heydrich for the Nazi party, urged him to join the Nazi SS, and became his wife.

Still only twenty-seven, he scored an interview with Heinrich Himmler, the Reichsführer-SS (commander) who challenged Heydrich to develop a detailed plan for an SS intelligence-gathering service in twenty minutes or less. Impressed by the impromptu written plan Heydrich developed, not to mention his self-confidence and "Aryan looks" whatever that meant, Himmler assigned Heydrich to create and implement a new organization called the SS Security Service.

Working at the proverbial bare desk with an old typewriter in a small office, Heydrich organized "a vast network of informers that developed dossiers on anyone who might oppose Hitler." He also conducted internal espionage and investigations to gather the smallest details about Nazi members and leaders.

Heydrich became an SS major by December 1931, a colonel seven months later, and, wonder of wonders, an SS brigadier general in March 1933, before his thirtieth birthday. One only can speculate on whether the dossiers he developed on top Nazis through the clever use of hidden cameras and microphones lightened his burden as he rose to the top. Whether by design or through idle talk, the supposed Jewish ancestry rumors that had plagued Heydrich since childhood returned again. This time the rumors, supported in part by the discovery that his paternal grandmother, once widowed, married a man with a "Jewish sounding surname," came to the attention of Himmler, who considered expelling Heydrich from the SS. Hitler, of all people, came to the rescue after a long personal interview with Heydrich, later saying, in effect, that the young man was so inherently dangerous that it would be safest to keep him in the party. That said, the rumors about his background persisted, fostering Heydrich's ever-increasing hostility toward Jews, even as he became ever more insecure. On one occasion after a night of drinking, he turned on a light in his apartment, saw his own reflection in a hall mirror, and shot the mirror twice, or so the story goes.

Once Hitler and the Nazis came to power in January 1933 through a series of elections and appointments, Heydrich and Himmler began arresting communists, Catholic political leaders, and trade unionists who had opposed them. An abandoned munitions factory at Dachau, fifteen miles northwest of Munich, became a concentration camp for political prisoners. During those early days, political prisoners who formally submitted to Nazi control were eventually released. Larger SS concentration camps followed at Buchenwald and elsewhere, but in June 1934 Heydrich became part of a tripartite that challenged then-powerful SA (Stormtroopers) chief Ernst Röhm in a high-risk, all-or-nothing power play.

Himmler, Heydrich, and Hermann Göring spread a rumor that Röhm would soon order his four million SA (not SS) storm troopers to seize control of the government and place Röhm in control. Having persuaded Hitler that Röhm must be killed, Heydrich prepared a list of SA leaders who were to be hunted down and eliminated on Saturday, June 30, 1934.

Three years later Heydrich somehow persuaded Joseph Stalin to purge several top Soviet generals by providing Stalin evidence of a threatened military coup by the former chief of general staff Red Army General Headquarters, Marshal M. Tukhachevsky, and seven other generals.

Stalin had them all arrested in mid-June 1937 on announced charges of making unauthorized and "anti-state" contacts with the military forces of foreign countries actively pursuing anti-Soviet policies. The Soviet government charged them with acts of treason as well as violations of their military oaths. Tukhachevsky and the others were part of a conspiracy to substitute capitalism and free land ownership for the communist system by establishing contacts and relationships among anti-Soviet. The accused men furthered the plot by conducting military espionage. When placed before the Supreme Court of the USSR, they all confessed, or so it was alleged. Radio Moscow announced all this and more.

Heydrich played a critical role in this development after the Gestapo learned that Tukhachevsky and other Soviet generals were seeking to negotiate with certain German generals for increased military control over the war by confirming the authenticity of certain military documents the Gestapo had stolen from the Wehrmacht (armed forces) archives. He followed this by helping eliminate two powerful generals who had expressed opposition to the long-range war plans Hitler announced in November 1937. After the first widespread systemic attack on Jews began on November 9, 1938 with Kristallnacht, Heydrich personally signed orders sending some twenty-five thousand Jewish men to concentration camps. Two months later, in early January 1939, Heydrich sent a sabotage team into Slovakia, a province in eastern Czechoslovakia, in advance of the March 1939 German army invasion of that country.

He also manufactured a September 1, 1939 Polish attack on a German radio station at Gleiwitz on the border between the two countries. That incident created the pretext for the German invasion of Poland, plunging Europe into war.

Hitler rewarded Heydrich for the Gleiwitz incident by placing him in charge of the newly created Reich Main Security Office, known in Germany by the acronym RSHA, combining the SS Security Service, known in Germany as the SD; the Gestapo; the Criminal Police, which investigated ordinary criminal matters; and the foreign intelligence service. Those organizational details settled, Heydrich then developed and implemented a plan for the destruction of Poland to meet Hitler's then-current strategic objectives.

Heydrich created five SS special action (Einsatz) groups to execute unarmed Polish politicians, clergy, and leading citizens, paving the way, the Nazis hoped, for the permanent enslavement of everyone else in that country. Heydrich ordered the execution or ghetto confinement of the Jewish population in Warsaw, Kraków, and Lodz. Some five hundred thousand Polish Jews subjected to this policy died by June 1941. That very month Germany turned on its Russian allies and invaded the Soviet Union, killing all communist political commissars, partisans, and others assessed as security threats along the road to Moscow, even as volunteer units of ethnic Germans living in Poland, Latvia, Lithuania, and Ukraine joined the procession to the outskirts of Moscow. The Russians stopped them thirteen miles outside the city.

Throughout all of Nazi-occupied Europe, Einsatz elements commanded by Heydrich systemized the slaughter of Jews, as the coward Otto Ohlendorf Nazi Gruppenfuhrer (high ranking SA officer) described during his Nuremberg trial. The devious routine used to carry out this genocide called for going into towns, villages, or even cities, calling out Jewish leaders, and then persuading them that a resettlement rather than a slaughter was about to be carried out. At the last minute, all the victims were asked to hand over their valuables for "safekeeping" just before they were stripped of all clothing, led to the place of execution, and then shot. All the bodies, dead or otherwise, were thrown into a nearby ditch.

Now these miscreants stood accused of breaking their military allegiance oaths, violating duties they were sworn to perform, and working against the

Soviet Union on behalf of a foreign country. More specifically, while working with foreign military officials, they had helped organize an *anti-Soviet* organization while conducting military espionage against the Red Army, all with the goal of helping defeat the Red Army if and when the Soviet Union was attacked. Worse still, the accused carried out these objectives on behalf of "big land ownership and capitalism." Perhaps no one should be surprised that Soviet persuasion guided them all into confessing.

Through Nazi criminal Hermann Göring, Hitler directed Heydrich in July 1941 to prepare "a general plan of the administrative material and financial measures necessary for carrying out the desired final solution of the Jewish question." Heydrich convened a conference of some fifteen top Nazi administrators for that purpose in Wannsee, near Berlin, on Tuesday, January 20, 1942. Heydrich announced at the beginning of the conference: "Europe will be combed of Jews from east to west." Adolf Eichmann, one of the most "prominent" Nazi criminals captured after the war, recorded the minutes of the Wannsee Conference. "Instead of emigration," Eichmann recorded, "there is now a further possible solution which the Fuehrer has already signified his consent [sic]—namely deportation to the East." Mass gassings began at Auschwitz, Poland that June.

Four months earlier, in September 1941, Heydrich became the "Deputy Reich Protector of Bohemia and Moravia," in what only months before had been Czechoslovakia. All too soon he located a country home just outside Prague from which he directed periodic actions against the Czech resistance movement. This was in sharp contrast to his "whip and sugar" policy, as described in *The Secret History of World War II: Spies, Code Breakers, & Covert Operations* by Neil Kagan and Stephen G. Hyslop, one of the principal sources quoted where indicated in this chapter. "The sugar consisted of increased rations and benefits for Czech workers whose output at factories like the sprawling Skoda munitions plant helped sustain the ongoing German offensive in Russia." Industrial sabotage declined under Heydrich and production increased, in part because those incentives appeased workers but also because they feared the whip he wielded. After taking power, he declared martial law and had thousands of people arrested over the next few months. Some were active resisters, loyal to the Czech government-in-exile in London, but many were simply influential figures who might potentially cause trouble and encourage opposition. Here, as in Poland, the SS systematically eliminated those who were capable of exercising independent leadership, leaving only the collaborators in office. More than four hundred Czechs were executed during the Heydrich crackdown, and several thousand others were sent to concentration camps. Heydrich did everything possible to keep the ongoing Jewish Holocaust under wraps, employing a fictional "resettlement in the East" to minimize Jewish resistance and to keep "other non-Aryans, including millions of Slavic Czechs, Slovaks and Poles from recognizing that they too were menaced by their Nazi overseers, who viewed them as subhuman." Heydrich and Hitler planned postwar extermination for those Czechs too racially impure to "Germanize."

All of this caught the attention of Edvard Beneš, the former Czech president who now led the London-based government-in-exile. Beneš controlled (more or less) a three thousand–man army that shared his exile in England. Better yet, his military intelligence operation portfolio included one Paul Thümmel, an advantageously positioned German officer in Prague hiding behind the words and deeds of a Nazi extremist. Thümmel was somewhat controversial among Czech officials monitoring events from London. "Thümmel betrayed German war plans for small payments, raising questions in London about his true motives. Some suspected he was a double agent, feeding the Czechs false leads." That said, as recorded in *Secret History*, "his reports—including one in May 1941 detailing German preparations for the invasion of Russia—proved so accurate and valuable that the Allies concluded he was a real catch and gave Beneš credit for hooking him."

Inexplicably, a few days after Heydrich assumed his position in Prague, Thümmel stopped sending radio messages to London. Beneš began returning Czech soldiers as parachutists but decided to bolster his credibility with the Allied Powers in a bold stroke. Beneš proposed Operation Anthropoid, an action by his trained paratroop commandos to assassinate Heydrich, to be carried out in complete secrecy, not only to avoid alerting the German forces, but as a means of concealing the involvement of the government-in-exile and the British Special Operations Executive (SOE). Were the Germans to learn that the government-in-exile participated in such an assassination, Nazi retaliation against unarmed men, women, and children would quickly follow.

Neither Beneš nor the British wanted this to be seen as a plot concocted in London, even if it succeeded. The Germans had recently avenged the assassination of a local commander in France by killing fifty hostages. They were sure to exact a much heavier toll for an assault on Heydrich. Any credit or blame for the operation would be assigned by the organizers in London to homegrown Czech patriots acting spontaneously in defense of their country.

The backgrounds of the two Czech men selected for this mission, as described in *Secret History*, fit the bill perfectly.

The plan largely relied upon two Czech men who fought the Hun in France after fleeing Czechoslovakia. Jozef Gabčík and Jon Kubiš were sent to British for British SOE commando training deep in the Scottish Highlands. The course curricula included parachute training and the intricacies of killing Germans as silently as possible. Kubiš had been a second choice. He was selected only after the man chosen first injured himself in a hard parachute landing. That said, both Gabčík and Kubiš were strictly volunteers who agreed to take on a difficult task. Beneš and his intelligence chief, Lieutenant Colonel František Moravec, met briefly with the two men in London to point out the overwhelming importance of this do-or-die mission. One account says Beneš sent them off with tears in his eyes, understanding after the conversation that Gabčík and Kubiš accepted their fate, whatever that might be.

They flew toward the mission in the evening darkness of Wednesday, December 28, 1941 aboard a Halifax bomber with a range of 1,860 miles customized to deliver parachutists. Two teams of commandos responsible for reestablishing radio communications with Czech Resistance leaders who were to be dropped at separate landing zones were also on board. Although the drops were routine, Gabčík limped into the darkness with a newly injured foot. They considered themselves lucky that Nazi-affiliated police didn't see them. Eventually the Gabčík team found its way to a Prague safe house, thanks to assistance from Czech Resistance men who heard rumors of their landing and found them. Having gone that far, they were forced to disobey direct orders, although for good reasons that their superiors surely would have endorsed. They took Ladislav Vanek, leader of the specific Czech Resistance group hiding them into their confidence, relating their specific mission and seeking his assistance. Vanek helped them conduct surveillance, identify Heydrich's movements, and target the Nazi for assassination.

Soon, Czech Resistance headquarters back in London directed one of the two recently arrived radio teams to find the Anthropoid team.

Late February 1942 found Gabčík still limping along, nursing his injury from the parachuting accident that beset him two months before. A vast number of Czech informants eagerly provided information about Heydrich's daily routine and vulnerabilities. Whether out of arrogance or simple carelessness, Heydrich cared little for common sense steps and measures appropriate for an SS leader working in an occupied, hostile country. Heydrich enjoyed open-air trips in a convertible to the airport and other regular destinations in his daily routine, often bringing along only his driver. This bravado reflected his confidence that he had eliminated all real Czech opposition to the Reich and had no need for an armed guard. This bravado echoed flirtations with danger in Luftwaffe combat missions that Heydrich flew from time to time, at least until Himmler discovered what was going on and took away his flying privileges.

Gabčík and Kubiš were ready to conduct the operation that May, but others were uncomfortable with the timing. Vanek, the senior Czech Resistance leader in charge, considered the movement to be in a difficult position, which well might be made worse by the planned operation. After all, Thümmel, the German collaborator, had been arrested, even as the most important Czech contact with Thümmel was killed in a shootout with the Germans. Several parachutists bringing radios, weapons, and other equipment to help the Czech Resistance were hiding, or, worse yet, dead. Most of the Czech Resistance was in hiding, a situation that would be made worse if and when Heydrich was attacked. For this and other reasons, Vanek recommended in a coded message that a lesser important target replace Heydrich, for fear that Operation Anthropoid as planned would risk thousands of lives within the Czech Resistance.

Vanek feared, and not without reason, that the Nazis would kill everyone associated with the organization, rendering the resistance totally useless.

At least Gabčík and Kubiš were still ready, willing, and able—in fact eager—to carry out the Heydrich kill. Soon they learned that on the morning of May 27, 1942, Heydrich would fly to a meeting with Hitler. Some sources speculated that Heydrich would then be reassigned to other duties in occupied France, eliminating the assassination opportunity Gabčík and Kubiš now savored. For this reason, they figured out the probable route Heydrich would take to the airport, then on the outskirts of Prague.

At last the moment came when they could see his car coming around a bend in the road that forced all motorists to reduce speed. Ever so carefully, Gabčík opened a briefcase as unobtrusively as possible, put it underneath a raincoat, and began assembling it, even as a few yards across the road Kubiš began preparing two bombs that would blow up when they hit the Heydrich car. Before they knew it, destiny was at hand.

Gabčík drew a perfect bead on Heydrich as his open-air convertible turned into a long bend at about ten thirty. This was a perfect shot, or would have been had the Sten gun not jammed, giving Heydrich a fighting chance to personally fight the Resistance, if only for a few seconds. Instead of ordering his driver to speed on as quickly as possible, Heydrich ordered him to stop, giving another Resistance fighter named Kubiš a chance to throw a bomb into the car. Instead, the bomb struck the side of the vehicle, exploding with enough power to wound Heydrich in the spleen. Even then Heydrich refused to go quietly, wobbling out of the car after taking a few badly aimed shots at Gabčík, who fled on foot even as Kubiš peddled to freedom on a bicycle. Days later, despite an operation that might well have saved his life, the world was rid of Heydrich on Thursday June 4, 1942, thanks to a festering wound that wouldn't heal.

By then seven commandoes, including Gabčík, Kubiš, and Josef Valčík, who served as a lookout during the May 27 action, were hiding in the catacombs beneath an Orthodox church not far from where Heydrich was mortally wounded. Hitler had ordered the arrest of at least ten thousand Czech citizens who would serve as hostages, but anyone thought to have aided the assassins were to be executed along with their immediate families.

Some thirteen days later the citizens of Lidice found themselves being scrutinized by Gestapo agents and SS security police after they captured a Resistance parachutist carrying the Lidice family addresses of two Resistance comrades.

No evidence was found that they or anyone else in Lidice had aided the assassins, but all adult males in town—nearly two hundred men in all—were shot to death on the spot or executed after being detained and interrogated. Several women were killed as well, and the rest sent to Ravensbrück, a concentration camp for women in Germany, after being separated from their children. A small number of those children were spared to be Germanized, but more than eighty were sent to Chelmno, a death camp in Poland.

The Nazi-controlled press in Prague publicized the Lidice massacre widely, emphasizing how the town had been reduced to rubble, warning everyone that punishment was at hand, as indeed it was. Hitler initially ordered a roundup of at least ten thousand Czechs to be executed. Yet somehow, contrary to these orders, on June 13 authorities in Prague gave the local population five days in which to turn over the assassins. Karel Čurda, an experienced Czech commando parachuted into the country in March, contacted Gabčík and Kubiš the next month, but soon thereafter tired of the whole Resistance effort. After some time hiding with his mother, he marched straight to Gestapo headquarters, negotiated a cash award, not to mention amnesty for his family, and promptly sold out practically everyone he knew in the Resistance. He sent the Nazis to the home of a woman who had acted as a courier. Having little choice, she soon swallowed a cyanide capsule, setting the stage for her son, also a Resistance courier to be tortured. The Germans then showed the son his mother's severed head, carried into the room in a fish tank. Among other things, the captured son revealed that his mother directed him to a nearby church where he could hide with other commandoes.

Himmler learned that the commandos were trapped in the church and cabled authorities in Prague to take them alive so that British involvement in the assassination could be shown to the entire world. The trapped Czechs had plans of their own, however. Weapons in hand, they moved from the lowest point in the church to the highest, turning the choir loft into a defensive position from which they rained fire down on German troops who attacked at dawn on Thursday, June 18, killing several dozen before Gabčík and Kubiš used their last bullets on themselves.

Nazi reprisals against the innocent—particularly helpless children—continued into September, perhaps eventually numbering more than five thousand Czechs—including three thousand Jews deported to death camps in reprisal. Only a few days after his death, patriots in London and Prague began asking themselves whether the death of Heydrich was really worth the price. Kagan and Hyslop acknowledged the validity of this question in their book, *The Secret History of World War II: Spies, Code Breakers, & Covert Operations*, while noting that, in retrospect, the assassination was a major milestone in the defeat of the Nazis.

Heydrich's assassination deprived Nazi leaders of their aura of invincibility at a time when they seemed destined to dominate Europe. And by publicizing the Lidice massacre, the Germans lifted the veil of secrecy surrounding SS terror tactics and made the Allies more supportive of the Czech government in exile and more determined to seek unconditional surrender and bring the Nazis to justice. "If future generations ask us what we were fighting for in this war" said US Navy Secretary Frank Knox, "we shall tell them the story of Lidice."

CHAPTER 5

Heavy Water

You have to fight for your freedom and for peace. You have to fight for it every day, to keep it. It's like a glass boat; it's easy to break. It's easy to lose.
—JOACHIM RONNEBERG, LEADER OF OPERATION GUNNERSIDE

THE SITUATION CONFRONTING THE NINE-MAN SABOTAGE TEAM IN SOUTH-central Norway was no mystery. Their target: Vemork, a hydroelectric plant just outside of Rjukan, Norway, built on an icy crag of rock accessible only by a single-lane, closely guarded suspension bridge. The Germans had scattered landmines everywhere around it, even in the surrounding hillsides. Worse still, frequent patrols, searchlights, and machine-gun nests protected the target. They had memorized blueprints and photographs before coming here. Their preparation also included practice setting charges and negotiating stairwells.

Others tried to blow up Vemork before them and failed. Despite this, the saboteurs were confident they could accomplish this secret mission deep in the rugged Norwegian wilds. Perhaps it's best that they didn't know how critical Allied leaders believed this mission to be.

Despite everything the team members knew about the operational details of the mission, none of them could explain why this particular target might be worth all their lives. Something called "heavy water" supposedly gave the Nazis what they needed to destroy half of London, or so they were told. Whatever was here to be destroyed, whether the importance had been exaggerated to get them on board or not,

> *they were committed no matter the price, which would likely include their own lives. From the start, they had known that the odds of their survival were long. They might get inside the plant and complete the mission but getting out and away would be another story. If necessary, they would try to fight their way out, but escape was unlikely. Resolved not to be captured alive, each of them carried a cyanide pill encased in rubber, stashed in a lapel or waistband.*

Dying, or "going west," as the expression went, might or might not be their lot. So be it. This assignment and others like it made their chances of surviving the war slim at best.

No one understood this better than Leif Tronstad, who devised this mission and awaited developments back in England. He had promised that if successful, these saboteurs would be remembered for a hundred years, without explaining exactly why.

The Norwegian commandos didn't know the background behind this mission. Perhaps that was best, because so much rested on whether they could destroy the water pipes in the dark, dank basement of the hydroelectric plant to delay the development of Germany's own atomic bomb.

German nuclear research paralleled developments in the United States, beginning in the late 1930s with a secret program a German insider called the Uranium Club. Nobel Prize winner Werner Heisenberg joined the team at the insistence of Kurt Diebner, a Norwegian intelligence officer, physicist, and military organizer who served as team leader. Unlike the Americans who used graphite, German scientists decided to use heavy water to control the fission (not fusion) process. Shortly after the April 1940 invasion of Norway, German scientists took control of the Norsk Hydro Vemork plant constructed in 1933 to produce ammonia for nitrogen fertilizer using mountain water, which now was being used to produce heavy water for non-nuclear purposes. That all changed when the Germans took over the plant, forcing the staff to dramatically increase heavy water production.

Early 1941 brought news of this development to British Intelligence in England, courtesy of Leif Tronstad. Introducing himself as the source of the detailed intelligence about developments at the Norsk plant that the British had received earlier, he promptly began training commando units for sabotage operations in Norway, with the support of the British Special Operations Executive (SOE). Neal Bascomb, whose classic 2016 book, *The Winter Fortress: The Epic Mission to Sabotage Hitler's Atomic Bomb*, served as a source for this chapter, tagged the SOE as "the ministry of ungentlemanly warfare." The SOE trained commandos for missions throughout all of Nazi-occupied Europe. Company Linge, the Norwegian branch of the SOE, recruited Norwegian exiles living in England for intensive training in Scotland. The recruits climbed mountains, forded rivers, and lived outdoors for weeks at a time, all in preparation for dangerous assignments back in Norway.

Vemork was a natural fortress, surrounded by the Hardangervidda, called "the Vidda," a high mountain plateau in central Southern Norway. This presented a logistical challenge, which the Americans proposed to resolve through bombings. Tronstad objected to this, because in his opinion there was a high risk of extensive civilian casualties in nearby Rjukan should the bombs hit liquid-ammonia storage tanks at the plant chemical complex. Second, Tronstad reminded everyone that the heavy water facilities were located beneath numerous layers of metal and concrete in a basement, which might well protect the targeted equipment from destruction.

Persuaded by these arguments, the Norwegian-British operation turned to commando techniques to solve the heavy water problem. A Norwegian scouting team, code-named *Grouse*, parachuted into the mountains near the plant in October 1942 and was supposed to be followed about a month later by thirty-nine British troops in *Operation Freshman*. The *Freshman* plan called for the British to rendezvous with the Norwegian advance party and attack the plant. Bad in-air communications and worse weather resulted in the first of the two gliders delivering the British team to crash into a mountain, killing everyone onboard. The second glider crash-landed miles away from the plant. The survivors were captured and later executed by the Gestapo, as ordered by Hitler in his October 18, 1942 *Kommandobefehl* (Commando Order) designed to punish the Allies for their commando attacks.

The five-man *Grouse* group, led by Jens-Anton Poulsson, survived mainly on wild reindeer while waiting for new orders, which came in early February 1943. Renamed Swallow, the group was told that they would soon join forces with the second invasion force in Operation Gunnerside. The second force consisted of six Norwegians led by Joachim Rønneberg. They would wear British uniforms so that if captured, the Germans might be less likely to retaliate against the local population, or so it was thought, for reasons which remain obscure. This time, gliders would not be used. Instead Gunnerside operatives would parachute in.

They took off in a Halifax, a heavy British bomber, during a rainstorm from Royal Air Force (RAF) Tempsford, some two miles northeast of Sandy, Bedfordshire, England, wearing white camouflage suits and ski caps. They squeezed in beside all their gear, which included an arsenal of simple plastic explosives known as Nobel 808, which had been developed by the British company Nobel chemicals long before World War II. Of course they would also carry detonator cords, primers, relays, and pencil-size time fuses. At seven ten the evening of February 16, 1943, the plane rumbled down the runway and lifted off. Over the North Sea, the clouds disappeared, revealing the moonlit water below.

The Gunnerside team had waited for this moment at Gaynes Hall, a Georgian mansion in the middle of Cambridgeshire, near a village called Perry. The English rebel Oliver Cromwell lived at Gaynes Hall for twenty-one years. The first four days brought the unwelcome message, "No operation today." Then, rainstorm or not, they were on their way.

Soon the team was on the ground burying their parachutes before searching for the containers holding their equipment, while Hans Storhaug looked for shelter. He returned from that task with good news. A vacant cabin sat only about a mile from where they had landed. In the midst of a snowstorm, they dug a trench, filled it with the containers they had collected, marked it with rods, and took a navigational reading to assure they could retrieve the gear when needed. The cabin he found sported a sleeping loft, a kitchen full of food, and even a fireplace. Their next stop would be a hunting cabin that Poulsson had built before the war, which he called Fetter.

They began skiing toward their rendezvous with the advance at Lake Store Saure, some fifteen miles away, at about six o'clock in the evening. Each man had at least sixty-five pounds on his back, not to mention the two toboggans they took turns carrying, even as a snowstorm began to build behind them. Soon Rønneberg realized that they were either moving in the wrong direction or had been dropped someplace other than the planned drop zone. All they could do at this point was return to the cabin. With any luck they would find it, despite the blizzard they were walking into.

Meanwhile, the Swallow team, already holed up at Fetter, wondered where their Gunnerside comrades could be, knowing that the planned drop, for which they had prepared lights, had gone terribly wrong.

The Swallow team considered sending out a rescue team for the Gunnerside men, but soon realized that such a search would likely be futile in this dense snowstorm. Just about then a miracle happened—the Gunnerside men blundered into the very cabin they had started from. While the others slept, Rønneberg took the first watch, wondering all the while what they would do after this blizzard subsided.

Just after dawn they broke the lock on a side room door and inventoried the contents. After finding a fishing logbook, they discovered that the cabin sat beside the very lake Rønneberg had identified earlier. A Norwegian shipping magnate owned the place, which he called Jansbu.

Now confronted with at least three feet of snow, the Gunnerside team managed to open the door just wide enough to see high drifts and large, flat piles and piles of snow. The rapid change from comparatively balmy England to this made all of them sick, to one degree or another, suffering from swollen glands, rheumy eyes, and fever.

February 19 brought the storm to an even more intensive pitch, keeping the fireplace smoke from ascending upward and choking the cabin. Rønneberg found that all this kept him from thinking straight, even as he realized that he had better check on one of the roof braces supporting the chimney. And when he tried to do just that, a sudden wind lifted him up and dropped him into a snowbank far enough away from the cabin that he couldn't see it.

Somehow he found his way back.

Monday, February 22, the Gunnerside men woke up to something that struck them as highly unusual. Their cabin could have been mistaken for an igloo, complete with icicles and snowdrifts all around them.

They began packing for an afternoon hike to meet the Swallow group at Fetter after visiting their cargo stash in the snow. Given the distance and steep terrain they had to travel to reach Fetter, Rønneberg decided to take only what was necessary. Among the six of them Gunnerside carried, according to Neal Bascomb, "only enough explosives to blow up the high-concentration plant (not the surrounding machinery) uniforms for the Swallow team, rations for ten men for five days and their operational equipment—weapons, hand grenades, shears, axes, field glasses, detonators, time fuses and first-aid equipment." And then, at about one o'clock in the afternoon came the complication.

They could see a figure in the far distance lugging a sled behind him, heading directly for their cabin. The entire team sprang out of the cabin with six guns pointed at the pale-weathered face of a Norwegian outfitted for winter travel. He claimed to be a hunter named Kristian Kristiansen from a valley due east of the Vidda. The proof was on his sled, where they found some fifty pounds of reindeer meat, some rifles, and a list of his customers in Oslo. Perhaps because he assumed they were working for the Germans, he claimed to be a member of Nasjonal Samling (NS), a Norwegian political party affiliated with the Nazis, but he had no membership card. After a few more questions, Rønneberg concluded that Kristiansen was telling them what he thought they wanted to hear in order to avoid being shot. In all probability he was harmless, but that didn't mean they could free him. Instead Rønneberg decided to use him as a guide, but only after they feasted on part of his reindeer meat.

The next morning, Tuesday, February 23, after a brief rest in a small hut Kristiansen owned, the Gunnerside six set out again, searching for the Swallow advance party. Within hours they were all feasting on crackers, chocolate, reindeer, and even powdered milk at Fetter, the very rendezvous point they had spent a week looking for. Rønneberg released Kristiansen after the feast, warning him to stay on the Vidda and say nothing about the commandos. Discussion of the dangerous raid ahead of them could wait until dawn.

The commandos took every inch of floor space in Fetter that night, but just after dawn that Wednesday, all ten gathered around the dinner table as Rønneberg rolled out the plan of attack. He himself would lead the demolition party, accompanied by three of them. The Swallow radio operator would stay behind at the Jansbu cabin and establish radio communications with London, while the rest of the men split into pairs. Knut Haukelid, second in command of the Gunnerside Operation, would lead the five-man team responsible for covering the demolition party. Now they needed to figure out the best way in and out of the hydroelectric plant called Vemork. Rønneberg took on this task, sketching out the plant and surrounding area. His map showed the town of Rjukan to the right, Vemork in the middle, and Lake Mos to the left. The Måna River cut the Vestfjord Valley in half.

According to Bascomb, the plant itself was on the south side of the valley, perched on a ledge. Eleven pipelines that brought fuel to the project rose along the valley wall above the power station at a sharp angle. Nearby, a railroad track running east toward Rjukan could be seen next to a wall. Citizens on the north side of the valley had access to Vemork via a single-lane suspension bridge some seventy-five feet in length. Much of the staff working at the plant lived at a small hamlet called Vaer, which was divided by the Mosvann Road, which connected the Lake Mos dam with Rjukan.

The group debated three possible routes to Vemork. First, they could cross the ridge above the project and follow the floodgates down to the plant. Because a permanent guard had been stationed on top of the pipelines and the area had been heavily mined, this approach was quickly eliminated. Second, they could perform a direct attack in which they would take out the bridge guards and go across relatively easy terrain. But if they were spotted early, they would face heavy fighting.

Their last option, risky though it was, probably provided their best probability of success. Going down in and through the gorge and back up along the railroad track would bring them to a locked gate just outside the plant. The good news was that this gate was not often patrolled. On the other hand, traversing the railroad line would, from time to time if things went wrong, leave them facing a six-hundred-foot drop into the river below with nary a tree or shrub to grab along the way. Rønneberg deferred a final decision pending a final briefing the next evening, Thursday, February 25, by an operative who had connections inside the Vemork hydroelectric plant. The briefing would be at a cabin in Fjosbudalen, a nearby valley just a few miles northwest of Vemork. The cabin would serve as the launching point for the mission.

Swallow team member Claus Helberg met the operative that Thursday evening at the Fjosbudalen cabin. There they discussed the number of guards, the guard rotation, and, of critical importance, security on the suspension bridge. Confronted with all available information, Helberg decided that they must go across the bridge, guarded though it was. And with that Helberg and the operative feasted on spiced beef and yeast dough before calling it a night.

The rest of the team arrived at the Fjosbudalen cabin Friday evening as planned. The cabin was far too small for nine men, so they slept in shifts. Helberg briefed the new arrivals, noting that machine guns and floodlights were mounted on top of the main building. Another pair of guards watched the suspension bridge. The guardhouse on the Vemork side was equipped with an alarm. Worse still, if that alarm sounded, everything in and around the plant would be illuminated, day or night, even as German troops in Rjukan were alerted.

The gorge was unguarded and infrequently patrolled, but the climb from the gorge up to the railway was next to impossible in the summertime, without the ice that would confront them that February.

One of the men argued for the bridge approach. "It was swift and sure. They would kill the guards, and then storm the plant." Poulsson and Helberg had misgivings, but in the end they agreed that the bridge was their best choice. Rønneberg doubted it would be easy, but he agreed that the bridge was the best option and sided with them.

Now Rønneberg pulled some recent aerial photographs of Vemork out of his backpack. The team identified some places to cross the gorge and hide before the attack. Helberg was assigned to scout the terrain the next day. He left for Vemork the next morning, Saturday, February 27, wearing civilian clothes even as growing winds signaled the approach of a storm. Passing by the village of Vaer, he discovered a power line running parallel to the road above it. This took him to a path down into the gorge, which he took down to the Måna River, which would be passable, at least until warm weather came. Next he looked for a place along the river's edge that would offer a decent path up to the railway line. A groove in the cliff provided a difficult, yet manageable way up.

Of course they hadn't figured out yet how they would escape. Surely one of the nine men going on the mission could get in position to set the charges, despite the thirty guards they expected to be on duty. Even though nobody spoke up and said so, most of them thought their real chances of escaping were thin at best. Most likely, or so they thought, once the mission was accomplished, they would be trapped inside Vemork or hunted down nearby.

Rønneberg went through their exit plan in detail, remarking that a climb up the penstocks would likely lead to guards, minefields, and probable capture. Crossing the bridge and killing the guards as they went would bring sure repercussions for the local population. Instead they planned to escape going back the way they came, despite the punishing climb, because the guards were not likely to find and follow them. Rønneberg allowed the team to vote on their exit strategy. A bare majority voted to escape using the same path used to attack the plant.

Once that was decided, Rønneberg didn't hesitate. Because they would begin at eight o'clock the next morning, he urged the team to get some sleep if they could. That done, Rønneberg felt a tap on his shoulder. He looked over at Kasper Idland, an overweight former mailman, and began listening to a rather unusual confession. Idland didn't complain about the problematic plan calling for the team to trek 180 miles to the relative safety of Sweden, but Idland didn't think he could keep up with the rest of them. Idland gave Rønneberg and the rest of the team the option of leaving him behind if they had to.

Haukelid and several others tried to relax just a few hours before launching the mission against the Vemork hydroelectric plant. In that tense silence, one of the men looked toward the adjoining woods. Startled by the appearance of a young man walking directly toward their cabin, he entered the cabin and sounded the alert just before the stranger knocked once on the door. He didn't get a second chance to knock, because Poulsson jerked the door open and grabbed the young man by the throat.

"Who are you?" Poulsson demanded. The young man recognized his captor. "We were in the same class at school, Jens."

Tangstad, the man Poulsson was choking, tried to explain through his gasps that he had come to borrow a shovel. Tangstad explained that "his fiancée and another couple were staying up in the valley for a couple of days. Poulsson told him in no uncertain terms that he was to stay in his own cabin with the others for the whole weekend and that they were not to leave for any reason. Tangstad agreed."

Once Tangstad left, the Vemork team wondered whether Tangstad really could be trusted. "Rønneberg decided to go over to their cabin and talk to them. Their assurances that they were good Norwegians and opposed to the occupation convinced Rønneberg that they posed no threat." He started back to his own cabin, turned around on an impulse, and shouted, "God save the King and Fatherland," probably hoping against hope that God would do just that.

All too soon the time came to launch the Vemork mission. The men skied away from Fjosbudalen at eight o'clock that evening, wearing British Army uniforms covered by white camouflage suits, for all the good that would do them if they were captured. The nine of them, Rønneberg, Birger Stromsheim, Kasper Idland, Hans Storaug, Fredrik Kayser, Poulsson, Helberg, Arne Kjelstrup, and Haukelid carried five Tommy guns, not to mention pistols, knives, hand grenades, and chloroform pads to knock out the guards, if they were lucky. Their rucksacks carried explosives, sleeping bags, rations, and maps. Cyanide pills were hidden deep within their uniforms for instant use upon capture. No one would live long enough for the Gestapo to interrogate him.

Down they went into Fjosbudalen, illuminated only slightly by a dim moon racing through the clouds above. Helberg led them through the boulders, pines, and mountain birch among the quiet whispers of their skis.

Despite all of the unknowns that faced them now, there was one certainty. The mission must be successfully fulfilled irrespective of whether all or none of them survived. "Destroying the heavy water plant was paramount. Each man knew what to do once they arrived at the target." They had practiced their Special Operations Executive (SOE) training many times on many targets. The fundamentals were many but easy to remember. The students, whose very lives might depend on how well they absorbed and remembered their SOE lessons, learned to keep their guns *unloaded* to avoid accidental discharges that might reveal their whereabouts to the enemy. Although some might be surprised to hear it, instead of being urged to quickly execute their missions, the students were advised to make frequent stops in order to determine if they had been detected. They were even instructed to take short steps, lifting their feet high in the air in order to minimize the chance that they might be heard. Executing the mission was to be performed by two demolition teams, using two sets of explosive charges. Finally, they were told to rendezvous after the sabotage, calling out passwords to avoid meeting up with the wrong people. It all seemed so simple, and this mission, if successful, would strike a mighty blow for Norway, once the men got to Vemork.

Down into the valley they went, carrying their skis on their shoulders, slipping and sliding among the boulders when they were not up to their waists in snow. After about an hour of this, they reached the Mosvann Road. And from there they could barely see Vemork, some fifteen hundred feet across the gorge, while listening to the hum of the power station. "To a man they were mesmerized by the winter fortress. It was no wonder, Haukelid thought, that the Germans felt they only needed thirty guards on hand to defend it."

They weren't there yet. Now they skied east along the road to Vaer, fighting snow, slush, and ice caused by warm winds while they watched for headlights that would reveal their position. The German army recently moved troops along this road at night, and there was the chance they would do so again.

After a sharp turn, they returned to the forest to avoid detection, following a line of telephone poles toward their objective, even as the drop became ever steeper. In some places, they slid instead of walked, risking a head-over-heels tumble with every step.

Helberg was among the first to reach the road east of Vaer, with a few team members just behind him, only to be met a few seconds later by the headlights of two buses. They scrambled to hide behind a nearby snowbank, even as the rest of the team in the woods above them held onto trees to avoid falling into the road. The last two men almost fell on top of the buses as they drove by.

Back on the road they all put on their skis and traveled east. When they came alongside an open field, Helberg signaled them to follow him, and they worked their way up seventy-five yards to the power-line track that ran parallel to the road. A short distance down the track, they stopped and unloaded anything they would not need inside Vemork into a hastily dug snow depot, including their skis and ski poles. They also stripped off their white camouflage suits—army uniforms were better suited for hiding in the shadows. It also was essential that the sabotage be seen as a British-only military operation to prevent retaliation against the local Norwegian population.

Rønneberg and Stromsheim each carried a pack with more than enough detonators, explosives, and fuses to carry out the mission. The men assigned to cover the explosives team carried an assortment of Thompson machine guns, pistols, extra magazines, and hand grenades, preparing them for the worst if it should come to that. Kjelstrup carried the heavy shears they would need to cut their way through any locks between the team and the target.

Within minutes Helberg guided them down into the gorge, each man hanging onto shrubs and branches as they walked and sometimes slid toward the Måna River. They reached the bottom of the valley, where they had to wonder whether this temporary thaw would cause the waters of the river to sweep away the ice bridges they hoped to cross.

Within seconds they found one such bridge that just might hold all of their weight at one time. Helberg led the way passing across it as quickly as possible, the others behind him, hoping against hope that they would not have to swim the rest of the way.

Helberg looked intently for the slot in the gorge that was supposed to provide their path upward. Finding it at last, he discovered that the six-hundred-foot climb to the railroad line above would be much steeper than he remembered, without any ropes.

Now it was every man for himself, as every one of them searched with his frozen hands and feet for sturdy pieces of the rock cliff that would hold him, if only for a few precious seconds. The climb became more and more difficult as they encountered patches of ice and snow, sometimes holding onto either tree trunks or rock outcrops for dear life, climbing a few treacherous inches at a time. Climbing just a few feet seemed a great victory, because the wind was blowing all around them, threatening them with a deathly fall. Winter or not, their own sweat soon made its way to fingers that were numb.

On the way up Idland almost fell 150 feet, because his left hand could not grip a rock that he erroneously thought might make a good handhold.

Instead, while swinging back and forth above an ugly painful death, he quickly looked from left to right for something, anything, firm and dry enough that he could grab. In those first two or three seconds, all he found was wet stone resisting his grip. Somehow he got close enough to the wet wall to shift his grip on one rock from left hand to right hand, weighed down by a pack and Tommy gun, which became heavier and heavier. At first his right hand found nothing.

Now Idland began swinging his body from side to side in a slow but widening arc until he finally was able to grab some roots with his right hand even as his left-hand grip weakened. He snagged more roots with his right hand and continued moving up. He had to grab some roots he could count on or risk falling to his death.

A half hour into the climb they still could not see the railway line, which was their next objective, even as they all began to tire, with wounded fingers, numb toes, and aching limbs.

Most of the men remembered their mountain-climbing training back in Scotland and didn't look down into the gorge. Two men admitted later they couldn't resist.

Finally, just after eleven o'clock that night, the first man reached the tracks and was soon followed by others all too happy to have reached their first objective. Now they rested next to those tracks, looking to their main objective: the fortress at the end of the railroad.

Meanwhile, two Swallow operatives assigned to provide radio communications grew ever more impatient as they listened to a snow squall blow around their cabin some thirty miles from Rjukan. Both wanted to be on the mission to Vemork, no matter how important their present task.

The SOE didn't exactly have a surplus of well-trained radio operators. That meant that such men, burdened with heavy equipment that made great targets for the Germans, rarely went on sabotage missions. Paradoxically, despite all efforts to keep such men out of direct action, radio operators suffered the highest casualties among SOE operators in the field.

Now, virtually within the shadow of the fortress, the mission team walked along the railway line toward Vemork knowing that the heavy winds and rushing water would likely keep the Germans from hearing their footsteps across the frozen gravel.

Haukelid could see a vehicle off in the distance, on the road his team had crossed an hour ago, but as he came around a turn he could make out two German soldiers guarding the suspension bridge that would be their first objective. Some five hundred yards in the distance he saw the power station and hydrogen plant with makeshift guard barracks squeezed between them.

Twenty minutes before midnight, Haukelid stopped the team next to a shed protecting a transformer. They could see the bridge and watched the midnight changing of the guard as they feasted on chocolate and crackers.

They sat down together as closely as possible, straining to hear Rønneberg over all the noises coming from the power station behind them. They went over the mission again and again, until everyone was tired of hearing about it. First in, the demolition team would knock their way into the basement one way or another. The covering party would watch for anyone who might detect (or guess) what was going on. Once the mission was accomplished, they would escape. Should anyone be captured, they would kill themselves rather than be interrogated.

Soon, the Rønneberg nine watched the midnight changing of the guard, observing that all of the Germans carried their weapons carelessly and seemed terribly bored. That was about to change.

Almost as if rehearsed, the men all stood up together at noon. This was their last chance to check their weapons, ammunition, and explosives. Rønneberg said what they already knew. The mission was only a few minutes away. "What we do in the next hour will be a chapter of history for a hundred years to come. Together we will make it a worthy one," he said, before directing Haukelid to move out with the covering party.

The entire team followed Haukelid as he followed the footprints to a point about one hundred yards from the gate, where some storage sheds offered safe shelter, if only for the moment. At twelve thirty on the dot, two team members broke the gate padlock with shears and opened the gate so that the covering party could go in before the three men assigned to take care of the demolition.

While Poulsson aimed his weapon at the German barracks door, Haukelid prepared hand grenades in case they were needed. The two men positioned themselves behind two storage tanks a mere fifteen yards from where the Germans slept.

All the while, the demolition men were cutting a hole in the fence some fifty yards away from the railway gate before snapping the lock off the gate, which led to some warehouses and outbuildings, so that the team had a second escape route if needed. Rønneberg made one last visual sweep for any opposition, listening for any hostile sound, relieved that the hum of machines inside the plant was the only discernible noise.

Now came the most dangerous part as Stromsheim followed Rønneberg across an open yard toward the eight-story hydrogen plant. Moments later all four men went around to the side of the plant for a view of what was going on inside. They could see inside in a few places where blackout paint did not cover the entire window. In the northeast corner Rønneberg confirmed that a single individual monitored the control room.

The team found a steel door, but it wouldn't budge, at least initially. A second door nearby was also locked. Rønneberg went back to the plant basement to see if he had missed anything the first time, while two other team members continued looking for ground-level access. Everyone knew that it was only a matter of time before a guard saw them. Thinking back on the blueprints he studied earlier, Rønneberg remembered "a narrow tunnel filled with pipes and cables which ran between the basement ceiling and first floor and out a small access hole in the exterior wall facing the gorge. Rønneberg thought that if the tunnel had not been blocked during a recent security upgrade it might provide an access point."

This would not exactly be easy to pull off. Rønneberg searched through the snowbank along the outside wall for the ladder he had been told led up to the tunnel. Two minutes later he found it and led Kayser up the slippery steel, hoping against hope that he wouldn't fall. The tunnel entrance, as it happened, was only fifteen feet up but was filled with snow. A few minutes later he began crawling toward the objective with Kaiser just behind him. Nobody else followed them. Several minutes into the tunnel crawl, Rønneberg spotted several water pipes bending left into the ceiling. Squinting through the small space Ronneberg could make out several high-concentration cells and knew from this that they were close to their objective.

Seconds later Rønneberg heard the sharp ping of metal, looked behind him, and realized that Kayser's Colt .45 had slipped out of its holster and struck a pipe. The duo went silent as a precaution, even though they were almost certain that the machinery all around them had masked the accidental noise. After a few minutes they started crawling toward the objective again. Rønneberg found an opening in the floor, looked through it, observed a large hall on the floor below them, and dropped fifteen feet onto the hall floor, hoping there wasn't a guard in the corner.

This was the very room that held the eighteen high-concentration cells the team was there to destroy. Nearby a sign read "No Admittance Except on Business." Rønneberg and Kayser opened the doors with weapons in their hands, only to see an old man with gray hair turn toward them from his chair. Kayser ordered him in Norwegian to raise his hands.

Scared out of his wits, the old man's eyes darted between Rønneberg and Kayser, even as Kayser assured him that if he did exactly as he was told, nothing would happen to him. "We're British soldiers," Kayser lied, as Rønneberg went around the room locking every door, implementing the agreed strategy that hopefully would keep the Germans from taking revenge for this raid against the local Norwegian population. Kayser kept up this line of chatter, telling a story or two about life back in England as Rønneberg unpacked explosives and fuses while studying their objective.

In a sense, this was their lucky day. The two rows of nine high-concentration cells on their wooden stands looked exactly like the replicas Tronstad and a working partner had assembled at Brickendonbury Hall, thirty-one miles north of London, the place where Rønneberg and Kayser had trained for this mission. "Each cell tank was fifty inches tall, ten inches in diameter and made of stainless steel. A twisting snake of rubber tubes, electrical wires and iron pipes ran out of the top."

What was the purpose of this contraption? They didn't know exactly. "Rønneberg did not need to know how the cells worked only how to blow them up. The eighteen 'sausages' of Nobel 808, each twelve inches long, set out in front of him would do the trick."

He quickly slipped on a pair of rubber gloves, which wouldn't save him from a strong electrical surge but just might help him survive a weaker charge. Using the techniques he learned during hours of training back in Brickend-onbury, he quickly moved through all nine cells.

Just as he heard glass shatter somewhere behind him, out in the plant yard Haukelid glanced down at his watch while keeping an eye on the guard barracks, hoping against hope that they wouldn't be detected. Rønneberg wondered how the rest of the operation was going, worrying in particular about the demolition team, which should have entered the plant. Any moment now, or so he thought, the guards would bring searchlights, sirens, and machine guns into action making this mission all the more difficult if not fatal to everyone involved. All Haukelid could be certain of was what was around him: darkness, the relentless drone of the generators, and the barracks' closed door. His eyes searched constantly for any sign of the guards who were patrolling the grounds, knowing he had weapons and chloroform to deal with any Germans he encountered, if, and only if, he saw them first. So far they had been lucky—they had seen no one, and apparently no one had seen them—or so it seemed.

Haukelid thought back to something that seemed as though it had happened just yesterday. He remembered the thin walls, broken windows, and bloodied floors of a small house some one hundred miles north of Oslo where Haukelid and other Norwegians stumbled onto some German soldiers who inexplicably refused to surrender. Haukelid and the others surrounded the house, killing every German soldier there within a matter of minutes. Some dropped out of broken windows; others sprawled life-lessly around the house they defended so desperately. Snapping back to the present, Haukelid assumed the Norwegian held Tommy guns and grenades and probably would bring a similar end to the enemy guards in the barracks standing in front of him.

He asked himself whether something had gone wrong. He wondered and worried even as elsewhere Stromsheim knocked a few more pieces of glass out of a broken window. Still recovering from the surprise, Rønneberg ran to help. Stromsheim and Idland had decided to force their way into the high-concentration room and were almost shot by their own teammates.

Seconds later Rønneberg cut the fingers on his right hand trying to help. He ordered Idland "to stay outside and block the light shining from the bro-ken window. The guards would surely come running if they saw it."

Then Rønneberg and Stromsheim resumed setting the explosives to the cells. Working together, they quickly finished and attached the four-foot-long fuses to the charges. After these were lit, the men would have two minutes to get away. The team worried that after lighting the fuses and mak-ing their getaway, someone might discover what they had done and snuff out the bomb. In order to minimize this risk, they decided, at the urging of Stromsheim, to initially light two-minute fuses to see if anyone heard them. If not, they would light thirty-second fuses and make a run for it. During the discussion, Gustav Johansen, a night-shift worker the team befriended some-how misplaced his glasses. "This was no small thing in 1943 when replacing these prescription glasses might have been impossible. "

Rønneberg rose and searched the desk. He found the glasses case and passed it to Johansen, then returned to his task, attaching the fuses with insulation tape. His right glove was soaked with blood from where the win-dow glass had cut him. But now Johansen began whining that the glasses weren't in the case. Rønneberg shook his head, went over to the desk where

Johansen had been working, and found the spectacles squeezed inside Johansen's logbook.

Now that they were almost finished, Rønneberg ordered Stromsheim to prepare for their escape. Even as they left the room, Rønneberg , Stromsheim, and Johansen heard footsteps coming down the interior stairwell. Was it a German guard?

When they confronted Olav Ingebretson, the night watchman flung his hands up and cried out in surprise. Rønneberg had time to check his explosives one last time. He and maybe some of the other Norwegians realized by now how far they were pressing their luck, some forty-five minutes into the mission. He quickly removed the blood-red gloves he'd been wearing and then dropped a nondescript pack identified in some accounts as a parachute bag right on the floor. He briefly wondered whether the explosives were properly set, assured himself that they were, and struck a match. He brought the flame first to the two-minute fuses. Then he barked at Idland, who was still standing outside blocking the window to get clear. Rønneberg dashed into the hall, counting down the seconds in his head. To the two prisoners he said, "Up the stairs. Then lie down and keep your mouths open until you hear the bang, or you'll blow out your eardrums."

The three saboteurs raced through the basement-level steel door and ran away from the plant as quickly as they could. They were only twenty yards away when flames burst through the shattered plant windows behind them.

Elsewhere, Haukelid and Poulsson were disappointed and unimpressed by the muffled noises they heard. Yes, they could see that the plant windows had been blown out, but had they risked their lives for only the faint thud they heard in the distance? They worried that the explosion might not be strong enough to destroy the objective. Was there a problem? What they saw next made them worry even more. "In that instant of doubt, the barracks door opened, casting an arc of light onto the snow. A guard stood in the doorway for a few seconds, looking left and right, before stepping out into the cold. He wore a heavy coat but was unarmed and had no helmet."

The unarmed guard slowly crossed the fifty yards or so between the hydrogen plant and his barracks, almost as if nothing happened. Staring up at the plant and looking down toward the broken basement windows, he acted as if he might have just heard a grenade or some other small explosion. Seconds later he shut the barracks door behind him. Poulsson thought that was the last they would see of the Germans in the barracks.

Instead, the same guard, now wearing a helmet and armed with a rifle, walked out with a flashlight that he pointed ever so briefly toward Poulsson or Haukelid, but not directly on him. Poulsson targeted the man with his submachine gun but shouldered it when the guard turned once again toward the warmth of his own barracks.

The saboteurs rejoined several other team members at the railway gate and bounded off toward safety, only to hear alarms go off at the plant. Within minutes the entire valley was alive with Germans. The Norwegians had a head start, knowing that the Germans could begin a massive search for them within the valley at any moment. They pressed on as quickly as they could, crossed an ice bridge across the Måna River, and began their desperate climb. Looking back, they saw flashlights moving along the railway line. They had been discovered. The two guards taken prisoner during the operation had described what had happened, as the chief engineer at Vemork realized that all of the precious heavy water held in eighteen cells had swirled down the drain.

Even then, the nine saboteurs were playing hide-and-seek with cars along the road back to Rjukan, knowing full well that in a matter of minutes they might see truckloads of German troops coming to find them. When they reached their supply stash, everyone put on their white camouflage snowsuits and began the ski trip alongside the power-line track, above the road to Rjukan. Alarm sirens became ever louder as every German soldier in Rjukan prepared himself to search for the saboteurs who even then were taking off their skis and hiking toward the comparative safety of the nearby forest. Once there, they found the road that would lead them to the Vidda, if they survived the half-mile vertical climb in the cold stillness of an early morning. They faced a series of challenging 180-degree bends in the road (switchbacks), each of which cost them at least fifteen minutes. Worse still, this bare path was dangerously slick in some places and covered with snow in others. Four hours of this brought them to the top, where they celebrated however briefly before returning to the protection of the woods, even as a storm began to build.

But it didn't matter, for the saboteurs had escaped. Most of them returned to the cabin beside the lake, where they slept for eighteen hours straight. Whether they knew it or not, these nine men had delayed the Nazi nuclear weapons program for several critical months.

CHAPTER 6

Alamo!

General Douglas MacArthur didn't trust the military bureaucracy—at least that part of it that was called the Office of Strategic Services, because the OSS had close ties to the Joint Chiefs of Staff. MacArthur looked to one of his own men for a reconnaissance team that could provide reliable intelligence he could count on, without Washington interference. He turned to Major General Walter Krueger in late 1943, but Colonel Frederick Bradshaw developed the concepts and ground rules for the men who would be called Scouts. This was an all-volunteer organization with an intense six-week training program designed to eliminate all but the best candidates. Larry Alexander noted in his book, *Shadows in the Jungle: The Alamo Scouts Behind Japanese Lines in World War II*, one source quoted in this book, "Men were dismissed not just if they failed to make the grade physically, but also based on their personalities. Bullies, loudmouths and individualists didn't last."

The Alamo Scouts were so named because they were affiliated with the 6th Army, code-named the Alamo Force by Major General Krueger, a native of San Antonio, Texas. The name honored the Spanish Mission in San Antonio where as many as 257 Texans died fighting for Texas independence in early 1836.

The training developed mutual trust, teamwork, survival instincts, and keen senses. That last quality paid off later, when several scouts found a Japanese camp by following the scent of a sardine can carried by an enemy soldier.

Graduates enjoyed the best of everything the army had to offer in the field. Those amenities included, first and foremost, the best combat equipment and weapons, not to mention tents, food, and even refrigerators when feasible, leading someone to dub their camp "Hotel Alamo." There was, of course, a reason why Alamo Scouts were treated so well. The six- or seven-man scout teams quietly went behind Japanese lines for as long as seventy days, using hand signals as much as possible. They wore camouflage beneath painted faces as they scouted for available roads, beaches (including tides and currents), fresh water, and any information that might be needed later. Of course enemy positions, numbers, morale, and movements were also essential. In addition to these duties, they sometimes went on the offensive, raiding and destroying supply depots. Sometimes, where circumstances permitted, they also rescued prisoners of war and civilian hostages.

Two Alamo Scout teams participated in the first mission conducted by the scouts in late February 1944 under the overall command of Colonel Bradshaw. An earlier mission, a proposed four-day reconnaissance on the northern coast of New Guinea, had been scrubbed.

Lieutenant John R. C. McGowen of Amarillo, Texas led the first team. McGowen had a master's degree from Texas A & M. He also enrolled in the Reserve Officer Training Corps (ROTC) before working in Panama for the United Fruit Company. McGowen enlisted immediately after Pearl Harbor and soon volunteered for the Alamo Scouts. Lieutenant William Barnes led the second team of Alamo Scouts. Barnes played football at the University of Tennessee, then the second-ranked team in the nation, before joining the army. Barnes trained intelligence and reconnaissance platoons before joining the scouts.

This mission, initiated on Sunday, February 27, called for reconnaissance on Los Negros Island as a prelude to General MacArthur's planned re-occupation of the Bismarck Archipelago and seizure of a large Japanese naval base at Rabaul on New Britain. Los Negros and Manus were the two largest islands of a 160-island chain known as the Admiralty Islands, or the Admiralties.

The scouts were ordered to conduct a one-week reconnaissance of the western portion of Manus. The plan was modified several times for various reasons before reconnaissance pilots flying low over Los Negros reported seeing no signs at all of the Japanese on the island. This was in sharp contrast to a recent estimate of 4,050 compiled by MacArthur's own staff. The powers that be now speculated that perhaps the Japanese had abandoned Los

Negros entirely. Krueger, whose order set the creation of the Alamo Scouts in motion, simply could not bring himself to believe that the Japanese had any intention of abandoning Los Negros, even though none of the Mitchell bombers flying just above the trees across the island in an effort to distract the Japanese from shooting American photo reconnaissance planes drew any Japanese fire to speak of. Krueger wrote that circumstance off by simply saying that "it doesn't take a genius to fool Japanese reconnaissance," before ordering Bradshaw to report in.

Krueger wanted more solid intelligence, he told Colonel Horton V. White, then serving as Krueger's G2 intelligence chief. Before Krueger sent in the 1st Cavalry, he wanted his Alamo Scouts to take a look. He ordered Bradshaw to make that happen, but Bradshaw had trouble deciding whether McGowen or Barnes would get the lead assignment. In the end, Bradshaw flipped a coin without consulting either man. Because McGowen lost, his team would go in, while the Barnes crew would serve as the contact team, monitoring the lead team's progress and providing backup.

Bradshaw turned to White, who did the briefing. "The mission is Los Negros," White told them, summarizing the problem succinctly. "The air force is telling MacArthur that the Japs are abandoning the place, but General Krueger doesn't agree. This is a two-day mission. You'll fly in tomorrow night, by PBY landing as close to the shore as the pilot can get you." The term *PBY* referred to the Catalina, an amphibious aircraft then being used in that theater of operation. "You'll go the rest of the way by boat." White told them there were two airfields, giving them the locations and assuring them that B-25s would attack each airfield at just about the time McGowen's team was landing. "Once ashore, recon the area to the Northeast noting troop strengths and defenses, if any. First Cav [Cavalry] which will go in on the twenty-ninth needs that information. Then get back to the pickup point by the next morning." White continued, "During the extraction, the bombers will hit their airfields again. If, for any reason, the Catalina can't get in to pick you up on schedule, it will return again twenty-four hours later and again twenty-four hours after that for three days." White told them that the insertion team would be carrying a walkie-talkie so that McGowen could coordinate the pickup with Barnes. "As always, avoid contact with the enemy if possible," White reminded them. "If there are no questions, get some rest."

Moments later Krueger greeted each and every man on both teams in his tent, reminding them that this was the first time at bat for the Alamo Scouts. "Don't worry General," McGowen said. "We'll hit a home run."

Maybe that promise was what kept McGowen awake most of that night. His handpicked crew began checking their weapons, assembling their gear, and blackening their faces at three thirty in the morning. Each man carried K-rations for two days, two hand grenades, a walkie-talkie, and their personal weapon of choice. His number-two man, Technical Sergeant Caesar J. Ramirez, was capable of leading the mission himself, if it came to that. The four other men were all combat tested. The oldest, Private First Class John P. Lagoud was twenty-nine years old.

Their two-hour trip aboard the PBY was uneventful, marked only by brief conversations and the glow of the occasional cigarette. The adventure began when they flew into a heavy tropical thunderstorm on the final approach to Los Negros. The wind buffeted the wings, and the most casual observer could see that the seas bordering the island were simply too high for a safe landing. Everyone on board noticed the quick flash of something above them. The crew confirmed that this was, in all probability, exhaust flash from a Japanese plane whose pilot was far too busy trying to land safely to have noticed the Americans just below him.

They returned to their launching point at Langemak Bay, only to return the next day for a late landing at dawn. McGowen watched the Catalina land on the water and then begin a quiet, increasingly slow glide across the water, expecting it to stop—but that didn't happen. Although they were at least a half mile from shore, the pilot told Ramirez that he would neither get any closer to the island nor stop the plane. The team had no choice but to deploy from the moving plane. And so they did, even as the "the PBY pilot pushed open his throttles, the seaplane roared off across the surface of the water and lifted into the sky, its prop wash rocking the Scout boat." Worse still, the bomber strikes they had been promised hadn't started yet. McGowen simply told them to row.

About half an hour later, the McGowen team reached the island. Gomez was the first one out so that he could help move a rubber boat across the beach. Months later, Gomez learned that MacArthur erroneously awarded a Distinguished Service Cross to another man for being the first man ashore at Los Negros. But now Gomez and the others quickly deflated the boat and buried it with a CO_2 cylinder under a tree and moved toward the Momote airfield, even as a lone Japanese soldier nearby began running back to report their arrival. Colonel Yoshio Ezaki, commander of the Admiralty garrison, quickly sent out patrols to find them just before shifting most of his troops to the west, many miles distant from Hyane Harbor.

Some three hours later the Americans, plodding through dense jungle, came upon something they weren't ready for: a series of vines strung from tree to tree about five feet off the ground. Ramirez had no idea what this meant, but McGowen guessed that this was a crude device to keep Japanese troops from inadvertently straying off of jungle trails. He also told Ramirez that this meant the Japanese were still on the island.

Just as McGowen said this, several short bursts of heavy machine-gun fire opened somewhere in the distance and abruptly stopped, even as the scouts quickly and quietly dropped to the ground. Now they heard aircraft engines aloft, the dull *boom* of bombs, and the unmistakable chop of fighter-plane machine-gun fire above them. Ramirez said that it was about time.

Now came the difficult part as the McGowen team ran as quickly as they could for two hundred yards or so from northwest to southeast, across a series of trenches, some two hundred feet wide and two feet deep, barely hidden by small branches and a few leaves. Because the shoveled earth next to the trenches was still dark, they knew that these trenches and the apparent machine-gun emplacements were almost brand-new.

McGowen led his men through footprints and discarded ration packages telling them that the Japanese were very near. They heard a sudden scream nearby, followed by the soothing voice of a Japanese soldier undoubtedly trying to calm an injured brother in arms. At the first scream, McGowen, on point, put up a hand signal telling his men to freeze, and they quickly did just that. The silence became deafening as McGowen wondered, with more than a little concern, where exactly the Japanese were. Then, as if from out of nowhere, an enemy patrol moving perpendicular to the Americans appeared less than fifteen feet away. Thankfully McGowen saw them in time to signal for silence with his hand in the air. Tempted as he was to hit the ground, he couldn't do that for fear the noise of doing so would alert the enemy and mean sudden death. Living statues that they were, they could only watch in sweaty fear as the line of Japanese in dark-brown uniforms passed on and into some nearby bushes, entirely oblivious to the bloodshed they had just avoided.

McGowen gave that Japanese patrol plenty of space. Then his men gathered around him next to a wide, swift-moving creek. It was about one o'clock in the afternoon. McGowen told the men that all but certainly an airstrip was on the other side of the creek. He saw no reason to cross the swift running water and risk a firefight with the Japanese. They had found what they were looking for and would now head back while they still could in relative safety.

The planning chairborne ranger who assumed the Japanese were gone was just plain wrong.

Moving as quickly and silently as possible, they traveled back through the jungle the way they came. Soon they were crouching down again so they could watch a platoon or more of Japanese soldiers making their own way down a nearby path. They wanted to avoid yet another possible disastrous encounter with the Japanese. More than once, individual men lost their way, if only for a few frightening minutes, forcing McGowen to order his men to resume their march with the hope that the lost men would catch up. They found the rendezvous point by six o'clock, still wondering where Ramirez and Gomez might be, only to look up and enjoy the relief of seeing that the pair somehow had found the rest of them. A short march to a point some thirty yards from the beach placed them where they would set up a parameter and sleep in, however fitfully.

Dawn found the team filling their deflated rubber boat with CO_2 in preparation for their scheduled departure. After that McGowen broke radio silence, at some danger to the team, in order to warn Bradshaw through the radio operator: "This island is lousy with Japs."

Another hour brought the unmistakable shadow of the same PBY they had arrived on, flying lower, ever lower, to the surface of the ocean, finally touching down, even as McGowan and the rest of the men quickly jumped in their flimsy rubber boat and rowed as quickly as they could toward their rescuers. Seconds later they realized their pilot had no intention of coming to a complete halt. Instead he kept moving through the water just slow enough that they might, just might, have a chance of clambering aboard.

Incredibly, the PBY now moved so slowly that the team led by McGowen easily rowed alongside long enough that Barnes was able to lock his knees, reach through an open hatch, and grip the dinghy bobbing along in the prop wash. That done, Barnes now became a human bridge that the McGowen team used to crossed into the Catalina.

The whirling propeller once again became a menace, but that didn't stop four of them from getting aboard, even as the plane made a quick right turn, blasting McGowen's hat off of his head as he fell headlong into the turbulent water. Somehow a team member named Roberts grabbed McGowen by the arm firmly enough that the team members on the plane could drag them in. While the plane took off, one of the men deflated their rubber boat for the next mission.

They were back at Langemak Bay by nine thirty that evening. One of Krueger's intelligence officers, Major Franklin M. Rawolle, immediately recognized the significance of their report and commandeered a PT boat for a quick trip to meet Brigadier General William B. Chase, commander of the landing force, on its way to the Los Negros invasion. Chase ordered increased pre-landing naval gunfire on the areas the scouts identified, even as Krueger ordered additional troops held in reserve offshore in case the landing force met overwhelming numbers. MacArthur, on the other hand, didn't believe the scout report at all.

The action, dubbed Operation Brewer, began forty-nine hours later at Hyane Harbor, which the Japanese had weakened in response to the scout landing. The Americans encountered very little resistance at first. The harbor was so peaceful that MacArthur briefly visited the invading force, but the Japanese rallied, requiring Krueger to order in the reserve forces he had placed offshore.

The Chase after-action report specifically acknowledged how important the information gathered by the scouts had been to the American war effort. They had correctly reported a four- to five-thousand-man Japanese garrison strength, despite the fact that the Japanese had spotted them. The Americans almost immediately and frantically searched for them the entire time they were ashore. Captured documents eventually revealed the fundamental reason the densely vegetated island appeared to be uninhabited: Written orders forbade firing on enemy planes.

The captured papers also revealed that Ezaki, "fearing an [American] invasion at Chapatut Point, where the Scouts had been spotted, moved a large portion of his forces away from Hyane Harbor where the actual landing was set to come ashore." One Japanese officer later wrote, "We were fooled." The Los Negros controversy promoted by MacArthur was endorsed by Lieutenant General George C. Kenney, then commander of MacArthur's Allied Air Forces. Kenney simply said that the scout discovery of some twenty-five Japanese troops in the woods at night was of little or no value.

About six months later, on September 9, 1944, the Alamo Scout Training Camp (ASTC) graduated a fourth class consisting of two teams. Lieutenant William E. Nellist of Eureka, California, the California National Guard rifle champion and the best marksman then serving in the Alamo Scouts, led the first team. Lieutenant Thomas J "Stud" Rounsaville of Atoka, Oklahoma, who formerly served in the 187th Glider Infantry Regiment of the 11thAirborne, commanded the second team, which included men from Ohio, Hawaii, a Chippewa Indian reservation in Minnesota, and others.

Nineteen days later, on September 28, Lieutenant Louie Rapmund, a colorful Dutch lieutenant sporting jungle fatigues and an Australian bush hat, approached Rounsaville, then stationed with their teams on Roemberpon Island just off the Vogelkop Peninsula at the very eastern tip of New Guinea. One of the local natives had told Rapmund that the Japanese were holding ". . . the former Dutch governor of the area, along with his family and a number of native servants, in a small village at Cape Oransbari on the western cost of the Vogelkop Peninsula near the Maori River."

MacArthur and his command estimated that some two hundred thousand or more Japanese were stranded on the various islands in New Guinea. The Japanese no doubt held an unknown number of Dutch and Australian hostages and were now using them as forced labor. The Japanese order of battle was estimated to consist of some two thousand soldiers, many of which were stranded around Cape Oransbari.

Soon after passing this information to higher headquarters, a party consisting of Rounsaville, Rapmund, a former hostage, and several others soon paddled ashore some six miles north of Cape Oransbari, amid difficult terrain requiring a march of several hours through the tangled growth. Once on the edge of the village, they began taking notes from hiding places, focusing on the number of Japanese soldiers, general layout of the town, and other details that might be useful later. Rounsaville carefully calculated enemy strength and the layout of huts around the village, not to mention the approaches leading to the village. That accomplished, he began mapping out a coastal evacuation route, along with the specific point from which an evacuation could be accomplished. He was disappointed to see an occupied Japanese machine-gun emplacement at the best potential evacuation point. This operation would be a more difficult than he had hoped.

Nellist valued his own team as much as Rounsaville valued his. The Nellist squad included twenty-four-year-old Sergeant Andy Smith, who earlier had been voted the top athlete in the 6th Army because of his superb basketball and knife-throwing skills. Private Galen C. "Kit" Kittleson, formerly of the 503rd Parachute Infantry Regiment, won the Silver Star for knocking out a machine-gun nest. The team included two top-notch Filipinos, Private First Class Sabas A. Asis and Staff Sergeant Thomas A. Siason. "Rounding out the group was Pfc. Gilbert Cox, a large man built like a defensive football player and Tech Sgt. Wilbert C. Wismer."

Nellist, who had originally planned to become a sniper, didn't hesitate when Rounsaville pitched the Cape Oransbari operation. They asked Lieutenant Jack Dove to serve as the contact. Dove put together a first-string team that consisted of Tech Sergeant William Watson, Private Charley (not Charlie) Hill, and Naval Machinist Mate 1st Class K. W. Sanders. Rapmund, who brought Rounsaville and Nellist the idea, would arrange for three native guides to meet the teams once ashore.

They briefed the 6th Army G2 on Monday, October 2. Rounsaville planned for the teams to be dropped on the Wassoenger River about six miles from where the VIP prisoners were being held by the Japanese Secret Police. He expected they would have to overcome some thirty Japanese guards, free the prisoners quickly, and get away as fast as possible, because some two thousand more Japanese soldiers were in the area.

Weather became a problem late that evening. Four PT boats departing from Biak were quickly turned back by a heavy storm. The next night a submerged log bent a screw on one of the PT boats, forcing yet another delay. Finally, in the gloomy, moonless tropical darkness of a five o'clock sunset on October 5, the PT boat quartet skimmed across the dark waters again, coming to an abrupt stop off the dark coastline at about midnight.

Rounsaville quickly ordered the boats over the side. They almost lost Rapmund, who nearly stumbled into the water. Fortunately, Kittleson grabbed his web belt at the very last second, allowing the team the luxury of rowing on beneath a startling crimson moon coming up over the eastern horizon. Rounsaville told the teams that they need not worry about being spotted, because Rapmund had arranged for all the native canoes in the area to be picked up so that no one could report them to the Japanese.

They landed on a beach no wider than a yard, meeting three native guides who emerged from the jungle fitted out in khaki shorts. Rounsaville ordered one scout and one native guide to take the point. As most of the teams disappeared into the jungle darkness, two men stayed behind and rowed the three rubber rafts back to the PT boats.

Complete darkness surrounded them, because the few strands of moonlight above them were entirely erased by the thick greenery above their heads, save for a strange light emanating from all the decaying trees and shrubs around them. The natives knew the area well enough to quickly lead the Americans away from the danger of exposure lurking on the Wassoenger River. Instead they trudged toward the target along a mud-caked narrow path, led only by a flashlight from the tip of a Tommy gun piercing the darkness ahead.

Two hours into the jungle, Rounsaville ordered all flashlights turned off. They traipsed off down a trail heading south across Cape Oransbari toward the Maori River, reaching their objective just as two rifle shots from somewhere in the far distance rang out, prompting the scouts to quickly take a knee. A guide said something to Rapmund, who told Nellist and Rounsaville that what they heard was probably Japanese soldiers shooting wild pigs for food. Even so, they waited a full fifteen minutes before resuming the march. "After reaching the bank of the Maori River, the Scouts held their weapons up and cautiously waded through the knee-deep water, just upstream from the village."

At about three o'clock that morning, the scouts found the village, profiled as it was by a low moon peeping out from the tree line, prompting them to all kneel, smell, and observe. The smoke they smelled was from cooking fires used for last night's dinners. At least they hoped so, because the success of the attack just ahead depended entirely on the element of surprise. Someone having an early breakfast could spoil everything.

Rounsaville wanted some insurance before they moved forward. He asked Rapmund to send one of the native scouts into the village to locate the Japanese and determine how many were there.

Rapmund nodded his understanding and whispered to one of the natives who once served as an orderly to the Japanese in this camp before seeing a chance to escape and taking it. While they waited for the man to return, they watched the village as a dog barked and a rooster crowed from separate places in the jungle. Within the hour the native carried three stolen Japanese rifles into the camp as the rest of the scouts gathered around him, listening carefully as the man whispered.

He reported that there were twenty-three Japanese in the village and five assigned to the outposts. The good news was that all but five enemy soldiers were sound asleep in a stilted hut within about twenty yards of a similar structure being used as a jail for the governor and as a headquarters. The remaining five Japanese soldiers manned machine guns and a single piece of light artillery on shorelines around the island.

That said, the real problem was the hostages, who were scattered around various huts in the village with blood-curdling orders to stay inside or be shot. The men understood that the Japanese occupied classic Nipa huts elevated above the ground to distill hot air.

Rounsaville took this in, nodded to signal that he understood, and told them that the operation would begin at four o'clock in the morning.

Rounsaville and the other team leaders now implemented a plan developed after an earlier reconnaissance, initiating a three-prong attack on the main barracks at the same time others entered the commander's hut, where they would either kill or capture him, eliminating anyone who was with him.

Rounsaville whispered, "Let's go," and they began.

The Rounsaville crew slowly and ever so quietly crept around but not through the village, stepping across tangled underbrush to reach the long Nipa hut that was their first objective. The space beneath the stilted hut was even darker than it might have been, surrounded as it was by palm trees and other dense vegetation. Having ducked beneath the structure, all Rounsaville and the others could hear were the unmistakable rhythms of men snoring.

Rounsaville stared into the darkness, turned around, and divided his crew into two teams, each assigned to one of the two ladders that provided entrance into the elevated hut. Each team moved silently into its assigned position, where the men would wait in the tropical heat for the early morning attack. The men moved up the ladders to quietly observe what they would be confronted with before launching the attack. Peeking through the mosquito netting, they could see a dimly glowing oil lamp that cast deep shadows. And in one of those shadows, a soldier clad only in an oilcloth was making tea. Bringing his weapon to the ready, Rounsaville nodded to the others.

When the long hand on his watch moved to ten, Rounsaville tossed back the netting and fired a single shot into the man making tea and then emptied the entire gun magazine into the slumbering figures in front of him. The rest of the scouts swarmed into the hut, greeting Japanese, who moments ago were slumbering, with glaring flashlights, muzzle flashes, and gunfire. Those few who reached for their weapons near their beds were quickly killed, even as their wiser comrades jumped out of the windows and made a run for the jungle nearby. Two got no farther than a nearby ditch where scouts quickly killed them. Two scouts chased the escaping Japanese, but for only a few seconds.

"Let them go," Rounsaville called. "Let's gather up the hostages and get the hell out of here before they bring back help."

Smith watched all this from another barrack some twenty yards away, as he, Asis, and Wismer huddled together looking inside another hut where four Japanese had been snoring away. They stumbled into a bookcase, of all things, on their way inside, but they were lucky in that none of the slumbering enemies woke up, at least not until Rounsaville fired a single signal shot to start the slaughter. Smith took out two men with his carbine, reloaded the magazine, and finished the other two off before any of the Japanese realized what the hell was going on, muttering, "Sayonara (good-bye) assholes!" Only one enemy soldier remained alive.

Initially the shocked and surprised Japanese officer thought to be in charge stayed in his bed, eyes wide open. When one of the scouts demanded in Japanese that he surrender, the officer pushed his mosquito netting out of the way and rushed forward with a bayonet. Within seconds he fell back on his bed, as dead as he could be, as another scout freed the governor the scouts were looking for, gathered up whatever documents they could find, and stepped out of the hut, dropping a phosphorous grenade back in behind them.

Soon enough the structure began to burn wildly. All of this had taken less than three minutes, giving the men extra time to fan out and search the village for the hostages huddling in their tents, wondering what the hell was going on. Rapmund called them out, assuring them that they might live another day, as Rounsaville sent a runner to Nellist asking that he radio Dove for the rubber boats.

Elsewhere, the Americans searched the huts and a Japanese radio surfaced. "A few well-placed .30 caliber rounds converted it into junk." In another hut, Smith discovered a table holding a gramophone and several 78 RPM records, all American, including one by crooner Bing Crosby.

Crosby's record, "My Melancholy Baby," slid easily out of the paper cover with Crosby looking whimsically to the left and on to the turntable that soon began the familiar whirl and sound that transported Smith, however briefly, away from the war, dirt, and endless violence. He envisioned St. Louis, the Gateway to the West, and its 111-year-old cathedral and the Mississippi River and the bridges spanning it, as he quietly propped his muddy boots on a table and let himself relax.

That rest lasted only a moment, however, as it was quickly interrupted by the unmistakable eardrum-bursting sound of Tommy gun rounds passing his left ear, thanks to an ex-con named Vaquilar, who had just saved Smith's life.

Smith didn't see the Japanese soldier who seconds before had been standing just behind him, bayonet at the ready. As that enemy soldier slowly began sinking toward the floor, Smith realized how close he had come to dying in that hut.

"Jesus Christ," was all he could say.

Just about then other team members were freeing the Dutch governor, his wife, and twelve children nearby. Also being freed were the surviving wives and children of male staff members who had either fled into the jungle or been executed. Rounsaville now had twice as many prisoners to evacuate as had been planned.

Once the hostages were released and every nook and cranny of the village scoured for that single scrap of paper that might make a big difference in the fighting yet to come, the scouts methodically moved through the village, setting every single hut on fire. The phosphorus grenades quickly destroyed the bamboo walls and thatched roofs in extraordinarily bright fires, as flaming embers floated by in the darkness and captives trudged sadly toward the pickup points and uncertain futures.

The assault might have seemed like it took hours, but it had been accomplished in four minutes. Still, there was a problem. Nellist did not hear the signal shot Rounsaville had fired as planned, much less the gunfire that marked the mission's success.

Among other structures in the village, a bamboo hut with a palm-thatched roof caught the attention of some of the scouts. While one of the scouts waited for Rounsaville's signal to attack, he watched a Japanese soldier emerge with tunic in hand, strolling casually toward nearby bushes where he no doubt intended to relieve himself. Another Japanese soldier, this one carrying a rifle, put a pot of water on a fire to boil, as another two Japanese men emerged and strode toward the bushes.

Nellist tried to be patient about this. After all, he waited almost an hour for the signal from Rounsaville before deciding he had no choice but to attack.

Nellist and Cox crept ever so slowly toward the cooking fire, until they were some ten yards away from their targets. Only then did Nellist aim his M1 Garand rifle at the first target and fire, tossing the Japanese soldier unceremoniously onto his back. The twelve-gauge Remington automatic shotgun Cox carried made quick work of the second Japanese soldier.

Kittleson and Siason leaped to their feet, ran forward, and cut down the other two. Siason saw an unexpected fifth man dive into the bushes, and, investigating, found an officer, pistol in hand, but too terrified to fire. Siason leveled his carbine and squeezed off three rounds. Nellist directed one of the men to make sure the Japanese were dead, search them, and take the two Japanese machine guns in case they were needed. Just then, a runner from Rounsaville arrived as Nellist raised Dove on the radio.

Mission accomplished.

During the course of the war, some 325 officers and men graduated from the Alamo training camp, but only 138 conducted missions as members of the 12 Alamo Scout teams. At any given time during the war, no more than 65 enlisted men and 13 officers operated as scouts. Their accomplishments were legion. "By the war's end, the Alamo Scouts had conducted 108 missions all fraught with danger. Working miles behind enemy lines, they are credited with killing more than five hundred Japanese soldiers and taking about sixty soldiers." Not a single scout was killed in action, although about a dozen were wounded. Their most famous raid in the Philippines, conducted at a Japanese prisoner-of-war camp near Cabanatuan in January 1945, freed 489 military prisoners and 33 civilians.

But that is a story for another time.

CHAPTER 7

A One-Way Ticket

Robert M. Trimble held on to his most unique World War II stories for nearly sixty years, refusing again and again for almost a decade to tell his son Lee about his experiences in the "big one." After all, his own commanding officers told him back then that what he did in those last few months was top secret, never to be discussed with anyone, ever. Worse still, from Trimble's perspective, there was the very remote, diminishing, but real possibility that his public telling of his experiences back then with the Russian government might lead them to track him down in Northern Virginia, even in 2006.

His story began conventionally enough, as described in the opening paragraphs of *Beyond the Call: The True Story of One World War II Pilot's Covert Mission to Rescue POWs on the Eastern Front* by Lee Trimble with Jeremy Dronfield, which serves as a principal source quoted in this chapter.

Trimble spent much of the war at the controls of B-24 Liberators and B-17 Flying Fortresses, heavy bombers that crews called "heavies." His more notable missions included "harrowing raids over Germany and France during the last six months of 1944. He withstood the horror of seeing his friends blown to bits by German flak." He fought the controls of his planes to return to base "with engines in flames, or worse, blown completely off of the wing, leaving a hole ten men could stand in."

Trimble arrived at his new assignment at the US Army Air Force Base at Poltava, Ukraine on Thursday, February 15, 1945, the day before the Battle of Iwo Jima began in the Pacific. Poltava hosted one of only three air bases that Americans were allowed to operate in the Soviet Union. Trimble was expecting to hear the details of the low-risk taxi driver work he had been promised, ferrying repaired airplanes back to England and Italy. Trouble was, his new boss, Colonel Thomas Hampton now told him that this was a cover story designed to fool the Russians. Instead, Trimble would be conducting a two-purpose top-secret mission with counterintelligence agents. First he would find recently liberated American POWs wherever he could and help get them home. Later, this six-week mission included Allied POWs from other countries and death camp refugees.

Trimble grabbed a quick breath of crackling cold air as he stepped off the C-46 transport to get a look at his new home, wherever the hell he was. The first thing that impressed him was a wind so cold and strong that it practically pushed him back into the plane. This wind didn't go around you; it pierced the body like a knife, making the bitter winters Trimble faced back in the Alleghenies seem tame in comparison. So here he was, on the Ukrainian Steppe at a place called Poltava, then a home for some 128,000 souls. Stepping off the plane, Trimble observed that this place wasn't any more attractive than it had seemed from the air. The pale, snow-covered grass stretched on and on out to the horizon in every direction, interrupted only by occasional ramshackle huts that gave every appearance of being on the verge of collapse and a large number of colorless bombed-out buildings. Beneath his feet was so-called "hardstanding," or ground surfaced with a hard material for durability. Here in Poltava, steel planking was the material of choice, installed by the locals "temporarily" until the steel could be replaced by concrete, or so the Poltavians hoped. All around him, Trimble could see paths covered by frozen mud.

The Germans had lost this base in September 1943 after sabotaging every part of it they thought might be useful to their enemies, including the barracks, runways, and outbuildings.

Some of the most savage butchery and fighting on the Eastern Front occurred in this region, most notably battles at Kursk and Kharkov in 1942 and the following year. Poltava itself saw some of the worst fighting. Hundreds of thousands, if not millions, had died here in what later came to be called the Great Patriotic War.

Americans had arrived in the spring prior to Trimble's visit to clear the debris and build new facilities. The overall plan called for Poltava to serve as a stopover base for long-range bombing missions to the rich industrial targets smoke-stacked in the easternmost portions of the Reich, far distant from Allied bases in England and Italy.

The success of American bombing missions did little to mitigate increasing British and American concerns about the fate of Allied prisoners of war liberated in one fashion or another by Russian armed forces that had begun sweeping across Poland. One American leader, Office of Strategic Services (OSS) General William "Wild Bill" Donovan, wanted to create an American presence here and spent months sending numerous requests begging the Russians to permit placement of American agents throughout Russia, all to no avail. Running out of patience, Donovan and his fellow American officers decided to simply work around the Soviets and accept any consequences that came their way.

Major General Edmund W. Hill joined the American Military Mission in Moscow late that year, mainly to serve as air commander of all US Army Air Corps units, with collateral duty planning operations for OSS mission drops. If the Military Mission in Moscow wanted a man officially not an OSS officer, yet intimately connected with the operational structure of the OSS, they could not have done better than General Hill.

Trimble knew none of this when he stepped off his C-46 into what awaited him in Poltava. He and several other Americans jumped into a jeep for a quick ride through dozens of Russian sentries to the American part of the base. One would have had to be blind not to notice that the sentries bore rifles with the threatening long sword-like bayonets for which the Russians were famous. He didn't want one of those bayonets, but he envied the Russians their heavy fur-lined caps. They drove by war-weary heavy bombers, transports, and a single emblematic Soviet bi-plane to the officer quarters for a sit down with Colonel Hampton

"Welcome to paradise Captain Trimble!" Hampton always enjoyed this part of orienting new pilots, but then Trimble began to go on and on about how he was looking forward to some good times in England or maybe even in Italy as part of becoming a ferry pilot. Trimble saw himself ferrying bombers to be repaired and bombers already fixed back and forth across Europe while other bomber pilots did the dangerous work. Hampton quickly burst that balloon, watched Trimble frown as he began to consider the implications of the news, and slowly, ever so slowly, twisted the knife by chiding Trimble for not noticing that the passport somebody gave him back in England identified Trimble as a US diplomat.

Hampton had more than enough ferry pilots. "Your appointment comes from the [US] Military Mission in Moscow. You'll be working with the OSS, Captain; you're going to be our agent in Poland."

Trimble bunked down that night with his head spinning. He was exhausted; it seemed like days had passed since setting out that morning on this mission. He'd experienced whole days of bewilderment, briefing, and suppressed indignation, but he'd been lied to from the very beginning. His former commanding officer probably didn't know anything about that, but somebody in the shadows of the upper reaches of the chain of command had arranged this. He had suppressed his first internal reaction—there was nothing to be gained by chewing out Colonel Hampton, who gave him one reassurance: "We're not going to parachute you into Berlin or anything like that." *Thank God.*

Then came the situation he'd been sent here to address. Even as the Third Reich began deteriorating under the stress of Allied initiatives, the Nazi brass began "releasing" war prisoners by the millions, leaving them to survive on their own in the harshest of circumstances if they survived the dozens of massacres described in rumors flying about. The Soviets had liberated death camps in eastern Poland, liberated the inmates, tried the Nazis responsible, and in one instance even opened a museum memorializing the victims. Yet for reasons that remained unclear, the Soviets were generally far less sympathetic to the inmates of forced labor camps, who were generally on their own after liberation. Poles and Ukrainians at least had some hope of getting home, while others far from home had no such hope at all, at least not in the beginning. Prisons filled with thousands of American, British, French, Dutch, Polish, and Canadian prisoners seemingly lined the border between Germany and Poland.

Joseph Stalin's Decree of the Stavka of the Red Army Supreme High Command, Number 270, issued in August 1941 declared that Red Army officers and commissars who became prisoners should be treated as criminal deserters subject to immediate execution, and their families were subject to arrest. Allied leadership worried that the spirit of this decree might lead to the mistreatment of American, British, and other prisoners. In fact, much of the Allied leadership came to believe that this was exactly what would happen if not stopped through covert intervention.

~~~

American and British officialdom professed a belief that the Soviets would treat Allied prisoners well, even as they began organizing supplies and transportation to support contact teams that would soon be sent to Poltava and other points inside Poland in order to find, organize, and protect American and British prisoners held there. The Allies planned to build or otherwise occupy holding centers where limited emergency health care and supplies could be provided, while the former prisoners waited for eventual transportation to Poltava for more sophisticated treatment and accommodations. The last phase of the operation would take the POWS home via the Persian Corridor or the Black Sea.

Recent experiences suggested that this might be possible but very difficult. Mass liberations in Eastern Europe began in August 1944 with the fall of Rumania. The American and Rumanian governments were able to quickly evacuate the Allied POWs before the Russians took control of Rumanian territory. Poland would not be that easy, because the Soviets were on the move, occupying large sections of that country and installing like-minded government officials. Even as Hampton laid all this out for Trimble, he wondered how on God's green Earth he, of all people, was supposed to do anything about this. To him the solution alternatives seemed obvious. "Either there would be a massive airlift evacuation of POWs or a huge diplomatic fight between the Allies. Other than maybe flying as part of the airlift, there didn't seem to be anything he could contribute."

Perplexity compounded itself as Hampton continued through the "big picture" assessment. President Franklin D. Roosevelt, Prime Minister Winston Churchill, and Stalin just ended a "Big Three" conference at Yalta in the Crimea four days earlier. An agreement that they all signed included specific provisions on POWs. The Big Three agreed that liberated prisoners would be fed, sheltered, clothed, and granted full access to repatriation officers sent by nations from which the prisoners came. Provisions were also made of camp inspections and evacuations. Allied prisoners were to be kept separate from enemy (German) prisoners for the sake of safety. That said, as a practical matter, the successful implementation of the Big Three prisoner repatriation agreement depended entirely on the cooperation of the Soviet Union.

Sure Stalin had signed the agreement, but so what? Allied insiders doubted that he would ever explicitly permit or cooperate with any unilateral American operations at all in Soviet territory, much less standard Allied evacuation and welfare programs. That said, the Americans at the US Military Mission made nice with the Soviets, while planning covert operations to be conducted as if the Soviet Union were an enemy.

Now came the closer. Hampton quickly explained that Trimble would serve as an assistant operations officer with responsibility for the covert operations that would be necessary to successfully evacuate American and Allied POWs. Officially, he would be responsible for aircraft salvage and aircrew rescue, a position designed to disguise his real mission: traveling covertly into Poland, contacting POWs, gathering them together, and leading them to safety outside Soviet-controlled spaces.

One thing was sure. Officially, Trimble was traveling under diplomatic immunity. Hampton explained that the Soviets would follow him wherever he went, even though in theory the Russians couldn't touch him without setting off a diplomatic incident. In theory, the diplomatic passport he held assured his safety, but as a practical matter put him under suspicion and in fact made him vulnerable to the suspicions of communist officials. His main concern when dealing with the Russians was to make sure that his true mission was never detected, which he could only assure by watching his Soviet hosts more closely than they watched him.

The next morning found Trimble holding on for dear life in the back seat of a jeep swerving around shell holes and large piles of rubble bound for Brzezinka, some twenty miles away from Krakow, the Polish capital. From time to time they stopped for supply trucks, artillery pieces, troop trucks, and ambulances moving to and from the front line. The sound of gunfire became increasingly loud as they traveled toward the danger.

Just before they arrived at Brzezinka, the rumble became a roar of rolling thunder. On the edge of the village, the grind and flutter of machine guns in the far distance could be heard for a few seconds at a time between competing Russian artillery booms and German shell explosions. Somehow the month-long Soviet advance had slowly ground to a halt a few miles from this very spot.

Trimble sat surrounded by Red Army soldiers in long greatcoats, sometimes covering white winter smocks, sometimes not, many of them carrying machine guns with round magazines. Tanks driven by women officers but covered with soldiers bumming rides buzzed by Robert's jeep, even in tight streets set among tall wooden houses that made this place look like a quaint storybook village long before everything in it was savaged by war.

Less than a day in the country and Trimble had already been distracted from his objective. He wasn't here to sightsee. The higher-ups back at Eastern command wanted him to put eyes on something and send them a full report. The Soviets also wanted an American to come here, which was highly unusual. Colonel Hampton saw this as a perfect opportunity to get Trimble into Poland without the "Russian stall" they usually had to deal with. Trimble was still in a daze, trying to think through the quick, complicated briefing he received, as he traveled through this unique and foreign land called Poland.

A Russian second lieutenant sat beside him in the jeep. Maiya, both engaging and beautiful, served as Trimble's interpreter, but the Russian Eastern Command probably assigned her this work in order to compromise Trimble or any other American who might fall under the spell of her coquettish smile. The army uniform shouldn't have fooled Trimble or anyone else. Maiya was a seasoned member of the NKVD, the Soviet political police. The NKVD, comparable in many ways to the German Gestapo, was there to spy on Trimble and compromise him if possible with sex. Wary Americans quipped long before this jeep ride that NKVD stood for "no ketch venereal disease." American officers assigned to the Russian Eastern Command called Russian men who did similar work, without the sex, "bird dogs." Her smile was contrived but beautiful.

That smile disappeared as they drove through the village toward the edge of town. Now she looked sad and wary, perhaps because she had seen what lay ahead of them before. Soon they would see wire fences with guard towers and brick buildings with rows of barracks looming in the distance, the fences stretching as far as the eye could see. The German name for this place on the far side of Brzezinka didn't sound familiar to Trimble, but the world would come to know it as Auschwitz.

The map Hampton showed him hours earlier had made it all look so simple. He was to operate within a triangle bordered by Lwów, Lublin, and Kraków, where he could expect to find aircraft crash-landing sites, if and only if he could depend on Soviet and Polish intelligence reports supplemented by interviews with rescued aircrews and plain old guesswork.

Hampton revealed that Trimble would largely be relying on operations officer Major Michael Kowal, who he soon would meet. That said, Trimble would report directly to Hampton and "Moscow," meaning two generals: General Edmund W. Hill commanded the American Air Division at Moscow and General John R. Deane was overall commander of the American Military Mission stationed there.

Trimble had no way of knowing about some important new intelligence. "Just two days ago, while Robert was still en route from Tehran through the snowstorms of the Caucasus a message had come through to General Deane at Moscow." Thousands of liberated American prisoners were wandering around loose and uncared for.

All the leads coming in from officers like paratrooper Colonel Charles Kouns and OSS Colonel Jerry Sage uniformly and strongly suggested that the Russians were not honoring Yalta agreement obligations, even as the Soviets themselves claimed all was fine.

Deane chose to act quickly. He assigned two of his most seasoned senior staff members to quickly drive to Lublin, inspect the Russian facilities set aside for American POWs, and then move on to any other Polish facilities in towns they could find where the Russians planned to "accommodate" Americans. The idea was to send every single American POW they could find on to Tehran by airplane.

Wilmeth and Kingsbury, the two American lieutenant colonels assigned to this task traveled from Moscow to Poltava with their very own interpreter the very day Robert Trimble arrived. The Americans had a "Plan A" and an alternative for the POW evacuation operation that lay ahead. Deane thought at this time that the odds were NOT in the favor of the Americans, although we don't know why in any detail. The original "inspection team" soon would be joined by POW contact teams, selected and assigned at the American Military Mission and currently en route to Poltava from London.

The Russian government helped bring Robert Trimble to Poland, but Lieutenant Colonels James D. Wilmeth and Curtis Kingsbury were turned back again and again. More than one American noted the irony of these apparent interferences less than a week after the Big Three signed the Yalta agreement. Deane became increasingly angry as the weeks went by.

Other American leaders also were concerned. Anger simmered in John G. Winant, US ambassador to the Court of St. James, whose son was among the prisoners who stood to be liberated by Soviet forces. Although neither Averill Harriman, the US Ambassador in Moscow, nor President Roosevelt had known relatives whose lives depended on the success of this mission, but they each considered the fate of Americans in German prison camps to be profoundly important.

Trimble knew nothing of this when he arrived at Poltava, and that was a good thing. Calling this a top-secret mission was an understatement. No one—absolutely no one who did not have a real need to know, even within military circles—should learn about this mission, either now or in the distant future.

There was a real need for utmost secrecy here, in that the Russian discovery of US agents covertly operating in bold defiance of NKVD and Red Army procedures might well lead to arguments beyond the usual niceties of diplomatic discussions. Indeed, some assessed an armed conflict between the United States and the Soviet Union as not beyond the realm of possibility. Trimble could rely on only minimal covert assistance from the OSS.

After his brief but momentous interview with Colonel Hampton, Trimble walked from one wooden shack to another for detailed discussions with Major Kowal. Fortunately, the two men had a great deal in common and bonded quickly. "Like Robert, Mike Kowal was a veteran bomber pilot. He had completed his combat tour with the 94th Bomb (not Bomber) group, flying B-17s out of Rougham, Suffolk, back in the dark days of 1943, when the Luftwaffe was stronger and the Eighth Air Force fighter escorts only went halfway to the target. Kowal believed in a brotherhood of bomber pilots, a breed apart from other airmen." He was two years older than twenty-five-year-old Trimble, but he had been an air-show stunt pilot from Passaic, New Jersey. His Slavic ancestry and Russian fluency landed him on the staff at Poltava in the early days of what would later been known as Operation Frantic.

Plane salvage and aircrew rescue coordination soon became part of Kowal's duties as assigned, duties that he relished enough to personally participate from time to time. Eventually the Soviets grounded Kowal, who they considered a loose cannon, more interested in gathering political intelligence than rescuing his fellow Americans. After bad-mouthing Soviet conduct in Poland in a missive, which the Russians somehow learned about, he was barred from entering Poland and restricted to Poltava.

Kowal soon gave Trimble a quick salvage and air-rescue briefing. "American bombers and fighters damaged in combat and unable to limp back to their bases in Britain or Italy often made crash landings in Poland. It was Eastern Command's job to rescue the crews and salvage the planes and bring both back to Poltava for transfer back to the crew's home bases." And that presented certain opportunities.

Aircrew evacuations rarely caused any problems, controversies, or arguments with the Soviets. After all, the Allied military men in question always wore uniforms, could prove who they were, and landed in plain sight of the Russian forces. Yes, there had been a few incidents in which Russian interrogators treated Allied flight crews roughly, but for the most part the Russians treated them as comrades, not spies. American plane rescue crews experienced little, if any, difficulty leaving Poland.

Aircraft were another issue entirely. The US government wanted all of the aircraft back as soon as possible, to keep the Soviets from acquiring expensive-to-develop technology that could be reverse engineered.

Kowal discussed this important issue with Trimble in great detail, stressing the need to get along with the Russians while at the same time doing everything possible to avoid American aircraft being stolen, scavenged, or destroyed. This was not always an easy objective to attain, because drunken Russian soldiers were sometimes encountered as often as Russian intelligence professionals were. Beyond that, even the Russian professionals were often tasked to seize American airplanes that had been repaired and were operating. American success often depended simply on which Russians showed up at a crash site.

During a follow-on briefing by Captain William Fitchen, the intelligence officer whose job was to interrogate rescued American aircrews, Trimble quickly understood that he and others on the same mission were, as important collateral duty, providing cover for the rescued American POWs. This gave Trimble and the others "a fairly free run of the country, albeit in company with bird dogs, and an excuse to travel to remote areas. It also allowed for intelligence gathering since the information about landing sites that came through the Red Army was vague and inquiries had to be made to find the exact locations of planes and crews." Under cover of this activity, Trimble's mission was to contract and exfiltrate wandering prisoners. Problem was, how was he supposed to get this done?

His next session with Hampton provided at least some of the answers, after reminding him that Trimble wouldn't be going to Berlin. The two men he would be meeting were trained to do just that. Next came meeting with OSS agents whose presence on the mission had to be covered up at all costs to avoid the possibility of a diplomatic dustup. Hampton slowly opened the door, and, after a brief hesitation, Trimble followed. The two men he saw before him were hardly James Bond 007 types.

Perhaps by design, the men Trimble worked with most often on such missions of this nature hardly stood out in a crowd; they could have passed as manufacturing workers anywhere between Athens and San Francisco. Their clothes were always nondescript, neither tacky nor fashionable.

"But of course this was their aim. Their dull jackets and coats, worn-looking pants and slightly frayed shirt collars had been painstakingly fabricated to German or Polish patterns at the OSS clothing depot in Brook Street, London, where they had the resources and skills to take anything from laborer overalls to a German army uniform or a Gestapo suit, using materials brought in from the OSS office in Stockholm, where German-made articles of clothing, luggage and personal effects could be purchase." Trimble never learned how the men got to Poltava, but one possibility was the Eagle Project.

The Allies designed Eagles for one purpose: to send agents to pose as skilled workers behind enemy lines to infiltrate German factories. The operators Trimble met with now likely were veterans of Operation Tissue, trained for one purpose and one purpose only: to infiltrate Germany. Their tasks centered on intelligence gathering, specifically focused on communications, surveillance, lock-picking, cryptography, and high-level forgery. Secondary emphasis focused on self-defense, rather than aggressive offense, in matters of direct violence. Once trained, these men were sent to Germany from the OSS Westfield Mission in Stockholm, Sweden, usually on ships that originated in Denmark.

Trimble learned that they were OSS men diverted from other missions to work as his contacts, quietly traveling deep into Poland, heavily occupied by the Soviets as it was, all for the purpose of developing relationships with local sources to learn all they could about the location and physical condition of Allied POWs. Of equal importance from an operational perspective was determining whether the Soviets could be counted on to help rescue these POWs.

These two conducted the first briefing as if it were a business meeting. There wasn't time to train Trimble the right way, beyond instructing him on contact procedures, codes, and a very basic system of communication protocols, which he memorized.

Trimble's lessons focused on field craft and outdoor skills that his teenage years in the remote Pennsylvania hills hunting deer prepared him for. Of course those years in rural Nirvana didn't prepare him for the second part of the curriculum: survival in war. He learned how to survive if he were being followed, including pursuit avoidance and throwing off someone following you, not to mention general survival skills.

Most important, Trimble had to avoid antagonizing the Soviets, most especially the NKVD. Should it become apparent that the Soviets were hostile at any level, it was most important that he not let them compromise him through the acceptance of hospitality or even transportation. Most important to Trimble, he had to operate in such a manner that risk of personal danger could be minimized. After all, one more dead body wouldn't be that hard to cover up in this war zone. "Robert's passport made him immune to arrest, but all the more vulnerable to murder."

Trimble could hardly sleep that night for fear that he was the wrong man to accomplish this mission. After all, he was a pilot, not an OSS operative. He could not see what he was good at that made him exactly the right man for the job. First, though, he had to deal with Auschwitz.

"What was unprecedented about this place was its sheer scale. The Auschwitz-Birkenau camp was vast. Beyond the gatehouse, the road and the rail tracks ran on and on." Eventually those tracks split and straddled a large station platform. "On either side, more layers of barbwire fencing stood rank upon rank of barrack buildings. Trimble found and picked up a poison gas can labeled with skull-and-crossbones and the warning, 'To be opened only by experienced persons.'"

Only a few hundred inmates remained in the camp. The Soviets and the Polish Red Cross did everything they could to alleviate or at least mitigate the suffering among the scores of living skeletons before moving them in horse-drawn carts toward hospital facilities. Only 4,880 of the 7,650 survivors liberated by the Soviets on January 27 were still alive ten days later. Robert couldn't help but notice that the Russians treated those survivors with great compassion, and he wondered whether what he'd been told about Russian indifference to the plight of American POWs was exaggerated or maybe not true at all.

He had no way of knowing that three prisoners arrived at the US embassy in Moscow that very day after a long journey by foot and train car across Poland, Ukraine, and part of Russia. Deane could only shake his head in amazement as they told the tale.

The three men were grizzled veterans of a camp designed specifically for officers at Szubin, a town in Western Poland called Oflag 64. Depending entirely on their own wits and survival skills, the trio set their own travel schedule, occasionally encountering hundreds of Americans wandering around looking for an alternative to the Soviet camp at Rembertów. They dodged the Russian "intelligence" men of the NKVD, while marching as quickly as possible toward Moscow where they distinguished themselves by becoming the very first escaped American POWs to debrief fellow Americans in often horrid detail describing how the Russians honored their treaty obligations to Allied POWs mostly in the breach.

Those intelligence sessions seemed to open a floodgate for emerging stories of neglect and abuse related by liberated American prisoners who somehow survived being used for Russian target practice, incarceration in understaffed and underequipped POW camps, forced marches dragging along seriously ill Allied prisoners, and desertions in the wilds of Poland.

For all intents and purposes, the Soviets treated victims of the fascists, such the Auschwitz survivors, with great compassion, but they had no sympathy for Allied troops captured by the enemy.

A few nights later, Trimble lay sleeping half dressed in Lwow, Poland. He had little to complain of that evening, ensconced as he was in a soft bed surrounded by polished Victorian furniture at the Hotel George, owned and operated, ironically enough, by the NKVD. Everything was peaceful until he heard the gunshots. Three drunken Soviet soldiers in the street beneath him had stuffed a woman into a trash can and were taking turns wounding her with their rifles. Seconds after Trimble figured out what was going on, one of them finished her off with a short burst, shrugged his shoulders, and took another drink. Trimble threw his Colt pistol on the bed, guilty in the thought that the Russian coward relieved him of the duty to act despite his undercover status. Later he learned that the Russians did the trash-can torture to any civilians they found on the streets after curfew.

Now totally awake in the early morning quiet with little chance of drifting back to sleep, Trimble began reviewing the random notes he'd transcribed from coded field-agent messages received from the US embassy in Moscow. That very night he would be searching for Americans hiding from the Russians in a barn, thanks to a brave farmer.

Dusk found him exiting a dilapidated sedan on a road in the middle of nowhere. Surrounded by forest, he used a tree limb to cover his footprints as he walked slowly into the trees, hoping against hope that he could find the Polish farm that was supposed to be in a clearing nearby. And find it he did.

Trouble with this farmer was the last thing Trimble needed; he moved toward the distant whispers coming from the barn only to be thwarted by a locked door. "I'm American!" he whispered to no one in particular after the voices inside dropped off midsentence. Soon the door opened ever so slightly, just wide enough to see a weary face illuminated by a single candle. Once again, Trimble assured them he was an American.

Mostly Americans, these men came from stalags (German prison camps) in eastern Germany and northern Poland thanks to Red Army liberators who arrived in late January. Once freed, the Americans were on their own; most found their way into the countryside. Although in the end, many returned to the POW camps out of desperation.

Somehow these twenty-three men found their way to this barn, where the farmer did what he could to feed them despite the almost certain death at the hands of the NKVD he faced should they be discovered.

Trimble dispensed with the formalities, shrugged the pack off of his back, and started handing out K rations. The lunchmeat, tinned cheese, malted milk tablets, pork loaf, and oatmeal didn't last long, so he began emptying chocolate bars and other treats out of his pockets before handing out the Camel cigarettes in a time when no one knew any better. He watched the barn fill with smoke as some of the guys broke into song, joined in a few seconds by nearly everyone. Trimble looked at some of the sick and injured, brought out his first-aid supplies for those he could help, and passed around a bottle of vodka among the rest.

When tomorrow brought the dawn, they would move out. The plan he had worked out was risky, but he thought it just might work.

Trimble was out of his bed in the straw well before dawn, taking two of the men who appeared to be leaders for a visit to the farmer. Despite the language barrier, the farmer understood and agreed to their request for a ride to the outskirts of Lwow. Trimble could see the farmer hitching a horse to a cart as he began assembling his men for the trip. Once the sickest among them were loaded, the rest of the men clambered aboard, settling in for the ride wherever they could.

They climbed out of the cart about a quarter mile from the center of Lwow, thanked the farmer for the last time, offered him money that he refused, and began the slow walk toward the train station and a three-day journey to Odessa, a major port on the Black Sea.

A grumpy Russian guard at the edge of town dealing with a hangover almost kept the Americans from catching that train. Trimble had his own passport, of course, but the rest of the Americans had lost any and all identity papers to the Germans long before today. The guard wasn't buying that explanation, however true it was. While the guard walked unsteadily toward the telephone to make a call to the city commandant who would undoubtedly order all of them into the Russian POW camp, Trimble quickly improvised. He offered the guard a huge wad of dollar bills for a half-empty liquor bottle and then waved him good-bye as they trudged on toward the station. In the weeks that followed, Trimble carried as much as $15,000 in his pocket, equal to $211,000 in modern money.

Minutes later Trimble watched the train pull away. With a sudden, almost painful clarity, he remembered the last time he had waved good-bye to someone on a train journey—his wife Eleanor, who he hadn't seen in over a year. "He wondered if he would ever see her again. He wondered if those twenty-three men would find their way home to the people they loved, whoever and wherever they were." Trimble had done all he could to see them on their way to freedom. How many others would there be before he was done?

Altogether, over the next six weeks, Trimble rescued or facilitated the rescue of over a thousand POWs, refugees, and concentration-camp survivors. When he returned to the United States after the war, he received the Bronze Star. Soon thereafter, the French ambassador to the United States presented him with the Croix de Guerre in recognition of his rescue of four hundred French women from a work farm in Poland. Trimble struggled with but overcame suicidal tendencies in the years immediately after the war, and he became a railroad conductor.

Some sixty years later, Trimble shared the story of his secret mission with his son Lee, in a series of interviews that began in 2006 and ended shortly before Trimble's death in 2009. But back in 1945, at the train station in Lwow, Trimble's hand touched the slips of paper in his pocket—each one a location, a number, and directions for the missions he would accomplish in the weeks to come.

CHAPTER 8

Azorian

THE CALL CAME EARLY THAT MORNING. CURTIS CROOKE, A LEAD ENGINEER at Global Marine, headquartered in the ornate Havenstrite Building in downtown Los Angeles, learned from his secretary that a mysterious man on the phone needed to speak with him about a large piece of business requiring immediate attention. Because Mr. Mystery wouldn't identify himself, Crooke refused the call but soon found himself confronted in the middle of a meeting by three men from "the government" according to *The Taking of K-129: How the CIA Used Howard Hughes to Steal a Russian Sub in the Most Daring Covert Operation in History* by Josh Dean, which served as a primary source quoted in this chapter.

While Crooke's engineers looked on, wondering how the boss was going to handle this, the government man who seemed to be in charge, about forty years old, thick in the shoulders but especially so in the middle, turned around and closed the door, signaling that everyone but Crooke needed to leave.

After Crooke's staff left the room, Mr. Mystery introduced himself as John Parangosky, presented his companions as Alex Holzer and Paul Evans, and confirmed that they all worked for the Central Intelligence Agency (CIA). He asked if they could sit down, no doubt understanding full well how much they had irritated Crooke, who asked for credentials only to be told they didn't carry any. Crooke decided to just let it pass, asking what he could do for them.

Parangosky had a job in mind for Global Marine—a job he was convinced from his own extensive detailed research on ocean drilling that only Global Marine could do. This was a challenging job, so interesting and so important that Parangosky had boarded a plane with his chief of security and chief scientist for this trip from Washington D.C. to Los Angeles, all to ask a single question to a single person.

Crooke nodded, so Parangosky continued.

"Is it feasible, using your current technology that's within the realm of possibility to lift something weighing several thousand tons from the bottom of the ocean floor at a depth of fifteen thousand to twenty-thousand feet?"

Crooke said that he'd have to think about it, so his three visitors left after Parangosky assured him that he would be calling back for the answer. Crooke wondered what exactly they'd be looking for if he accepted the assignment. The most obvious answer: a submarine.

This was hardly a surprise to Crooke. When the Navy lost one of its most valuable nuclear submarines, the USS *Scorpion*, and the ninety-nine sailors aboard her in late May 1968, eighteen months ago, one of the first places the Navy looked for help was Global Marine. The Navy wanted to know how best to neutralize the nuclear reactor still on board the *Scorpion*. Would it be best to recover or destroy what was left of the submarine? Crooke provided several proposals, the simplest, yet most efficient of which was to pump the *Scorpion* full of concrete, permanently eliminating any risk of a reactor leak. Crooke didn't get the job and still wondered why.

When Parangosky returned without an appointment the next day, Crooke told him he thought the task discussed could be accomplished. Parangosky said he'd be sending a work order and walked out.

—◦◦—

February 1968

There wasn't much fanfare the evening of February 24, 1968, when the Soviet nuclear ballistic missile submarine K-129 left the Russian port of Petropavlovsk on the remote Kamchatka Peninsula for a routine patrol.

Thirty-eight-year-old Ukrainian captain first rank Vladimir Kobzar, a man on the make, commanded the unimaginatively named Golf-class submarine PL-574. This was his last mission on this ship after a four-year assignment; Soviet Navy tongues wagged in speculation as to where Kobzar might ultimately land, but at the end of this final mission, he would be overseeing the command of numerous submarines from the boring safety of a steel desk in the colorless offices of Soviet Fleet headquarters.

The previous year, Kobzar received the prestigious Order of the Red Star, a ticket to better Navy assignments. This was no surprise, because his crews loved him and his superiors respected him. And yet nobody on board expected to be at sea that month. Following completion of a standard two-month combat patrol, on November 30, 1967, the boat returned to home port from the Northeast Pacific, only to be divided for their next assignments as was then customary. Half the personnel went on vacation, while the other half were assigned to routine maintenance: cleaning, painting, and doing repairs. That all changed when telegrams from Soviet Central Command ordered the entire crew to report to base no later than February 8. Getting K-129 ready for sea duty on such short notice was no easy task, as she was a relatively old vessel launched in 1960.

The submarine packed three R-21 SS-N-5 (Serb) ballistic nuclear missiles, each of which could fly 755 miles and carried a full megaton of explosives, more than sixty-five times the explosive force that turned Nagasaki into rubble during World War II. Coincidentally, the K-129 submarine could attack any location on the American coastline from positions that would be virtually undetectable to American military forces.

A remote, isolated station of sorts had been designated northwest of Hawaii in heavy seas filled with flotsam. Russian naval authorities directed the K-129 to proceed there and simply wait for further orders. Now and again American submarines hoping to stalk Soviet ballistic missile submarines would pass by. This K-129 had specific orders to stay completely out of site if possible and return to base by noon on May 5.

The K-129, a comparatively slow ballistic submarine considered highly vulnerable, cruised on an unerringly straight path, for the most part, punctuated only by intermittent, irregular zigs and zags employed as countermeasures popular during this Cold War era of naval hide-and-seek. Such measures were considered the best tactics available to shake any American submarines that might be lurking about.

Ballistic missile submarines carry intercontinental ballistic missiles, unlike attack submarines, which do not, because their mission is to hunt and kill submarines, with a secondary mission to attack surface targets with cruise missiles.

The Russian sub reached 180 degrees longitude and turned toward the US coast. Soon thereafterthe captain no doubt opened a packet of orders that directed him to destroy Pearl Harbor, US Pacific Command Headquarters in Oahu, and Hickam (not Hickham) Air Force Base, should the United States and the Soviet Union go to war. When K-129 did not call Soviet headquarters as expected on March 8, the Soviet Navy Central Command issued an alert. The authorities were worried, but things like this had happened before.

Soviet naval leadership didn't automatically assume a disaster when a specific submarine "went dark" for a day or so. Soviet equipment, especially radio transmitters, failed all the time. Sometimes weather could be a factor, not to mention the perpetual possibility of silence caused by US Navy vessels following or (theoretically) even attacking a Soviet submarine. Soviet admirals typically didn't lose any sleep until a particular submarine had stayed dark for more than twenty-four hours. The K-129 panic began only after the submarine had been missing for forty-eight hours.

No Soviet submarine with nuclear missiles on board had ever been lost. Command leaders began to speculate about what might have happened. Some considered damage to the ship antenna, collision with another ship, or a catastrophic fire, perhaps caused by a leak of rocket fuel. Some even wondered about an accident caused by low water salinity or other freakish conditions. Any of these could push a sub suddenly toward its depth limit, the point at which its hull collapses. The next day the Soviet command acted, sending out a virtual armada of ships from wherever they could be dispatched, with the hope that K-129, if damaged, would surface, send out distress messages from a predetermined area, and await rescue. This time the predetermined area only measured some 854,000 square miles. The designated rescuers were no doubt told to look for a surfaced submarine with little or no long-distance communication ability with little remaining electric power. At least they would not be starving, because submarines of that class carried at least three months' worth of provisions.

Bernard "Bud" Kauderer, commander of the USS *Barb*, watched an entire submarine group race out of Petropavlovsk with active sonar going full bore and wondered what the hell had happened. He followed from a safe distance, watching the vessels dive, resurface, and dive again while talking on an unsecured radio channel about the rescue efforts underway. The US Fleet Forces Command told Kauderer to stay put even as the Soviets increased their presence.

And that presence consisted of some fifty (sometimes more) surveillance planes following along the assumed path the K-129 followed, looking for something, anything, that might indicate what had happened to the submarine. Some thirty-six flagged Soviet ships joined the hunt. The mission continued for at least seventy-three days, consisting of some 286 flights over the zone surveyed, as two destroyers, two mother (command) ships, and ten surface-support vessels, not to mention at least four submarines, joined the hunt. It was a twenty-four-hour-a-day mission using photographic equipment to plumb the ocean depths, as echo and sonar sounders worked on the same mission.

It all came to nothing. About six months after the incident, the Soviets announced that K-129 went missing in the Pacific. Everyone on board was presumed lost. Yet Jim Bradley, a US Navy black operator stationed in Washington, saw an opportunity in this human tragedy.

The Americans had everything to gain strategically by successfully concluding such searches. Hard as it might be to believe, the key to unlocking untold mysteries about the entire Soviet arsenal—the composition and design of warheads and guidance systems—might well be unlocked by recovering a single, intact Soviet missile. American nuclear scientists dreamed of such discoveries.

Not only that, but Bradley had a pretty good idea of exactly how he could find K-129.

American naval intelligence considered locating Soviet submarines and knowing their exact locations at all times the most important part of its mission. This all began with the installation and anchoring of listening equipment called underwater hydrophones at strategic places across the oceans of the world whose mission included identifying enemy submarines. Belief in such programs as the key to maintaining the balance of power in the Cold War emerged in the 1960s and remained for decades to come.

Western Electric, a subsidiary of the American Telephone and Telegraph Company, designed the first hydrophone arrays. The first operational prototypes consisted of forty hydrophones laid out on a line 1,000 feet long and 1,440 feet deep off an island in the Bahamas called Eleuthera. When the system successfully detected a US submarine, a major system was stretched out across the East Coast and arched beyond that from the Caribbean to Nova Scotia.

After that, work began on a system of hydrophone arrays that covered the entire California coast, followed by a separate system in the Hawaiian Islands. The aggregated system, completed by 1958, became SOSUS, a contrived acronym for Sound Surveillance System, installed at a cost of 16 billion dollars, (140 billion dollars) in 2019 dollars.

Bradley suggested that the SOSUS recordings be searched for anything indicating where exactly K-129 was lost. When that search revealed nothing, Bradley went to plan B. The Atomic Energy Detection System (AEDS) had been developed in the early 1950s to monitor Soviet nuclear tests. Yet another agency, the Air Force Technical Applications Center (AFTAC), developed land-based sensors capable of detecting underwater explosions, initiated by Carl Romney, a Troy, New York engineer who worked above a cigar shop in downtown Troy.

Eventually, Romney relocated to Fairfax County, Virginia, where AFTAC is headquartered. That's where a Commander Jacob (first name unknown) from the Office of Naval Intelligence (ONI) dropped by to see him on Tuesday, May 14, 1968. "Jacob told Romney that a curious episode had been observed in the Pacific in mid-March: The Soviet Navy had mobilized an abnormally large fleet off Kamchatka, from which K-129 had departed."

The motley patchwork of fishing trawlers, cruisers, and submarines that someone might call an armada with a smile on his face moved ever so slowly in an easterly and then southerly direction toward Honshu, Japan's most populous island. The patrol orders then took the armada east along the fortieth parallel, eventually passing the International Date Line at 180 degrees east-west. Finally, and with some reluctance, they abandoned the mission.

Jacob asked whether the AFTAC staffers might have heard such a thing.

Romney made an educated guess, telling Jacob that his staffers probably heard something like that, but no available records could give them an immediate answer. Such an event could be identified by going back through the data and looking for it.

Monday, March 11, 1968 brought reports of a short but strong pulse detected in the North Pacific by numerous AFTAC hydrophones near the Aleutian Islands in Alaska. Because they knew the speed at which sound travels and could compare the times at which the detected signal arrived at each hydrophone, American military analysts could pinpoint the origin of the pulse with some degree of certainty.

Romney never thought that the explosion that seemed to come out of nowhere exactly 40 degrees north, 180 degrees west—as close to the International Date Line as you could come—precisely thirty seconds after midnight was an earthquake, volcano eruption, or an especially loud whale. This could only be a human event of one sort or another.

The second, almost identical signal came about six minutes later, well within the Soviet search area. All the Americans involved knew that this could be nothing other than the missing sub, still out there almost 17,000 feet beneath the placid surface of the Pacific, undiscovered by the Soviets despite their massive search effort. Best yet, it was 1,560 miles northwest of Oahu, Hawaii, a position almost tailor made for the Americans.

Yet there were complications that made the decision about whether or not to attempt recovery of K-129 no easy decision. First and foremost, there was no way to predict if K-129 was in sufficiently good condition to yield anything of solid intelligence value. Would they spend millions if not billions of dollars on the search effort only to discover that the interior of K-129 had been incinerated due to an explosion inside the vessel? Alternatively, had the hull crushed due to exterior pressure before crashing into the ocean floor, leaving a useless pile of junk? The answers to these questions could be answered only by conducting an expensive on-site photographic survey.

During the 1950s the American Office of Naval Research began tracking physics experiments conducted by the Swiss father-and-son team of Auguste and Jacques Piccard. Auguste, who sported wire-rimmed glasses and unkempt long gray hair, became prominent assisting Albert Einstein. Often called Piccard the Elder in government reports, authorities and experts considered him a genius inventor. One example was his 1931 balloon flight to a height of nine miles, doubling the existing record. His other obsession was ocean exploration.

First Auguste turned to William Beebe, a zoologist turned ocean explorer who built an early bathysphere, which is "a perfectly round steel sphere with thick windows that could hold two men and be lowered a half mile into the ocean on a steel tether." Auguste met Beebe at the 1933 Chicago World's Fair. Fifteen years later he launched his own bathysphere, followed by a second, improved version that he dubbed the *Trieste* in honor of the Italian city that had helped finance the project. The *Trieste* was twice as long as previous bathyspheres, but at this point Auguste ran out of money, only to be rescued by the United States.

He began working with the US Office of Naval Research in 1957 on dives conducted in the Mediterranean. Years later, investigators learned that the purpose for at least eight of the studies was to learn more about sound propagation—studies that were absolutely critical to the SOSUS hydrophone program. Eventually Auguste began working for the US Navy in San Diego, consulting on technical matters and training pilots.

K-129 team members also brought a chief navy scientist, John Piña Craven, into the salvage effort. Among other things, Craven led efforts to develop a Deep Submergence Rescue Vehicle (DSRV) for shallow-water rescue efforts and access to deeper waters for other purposes.

Three years before the K-129 incident, Craven reported to the Pentagon for a meeting about Sand Dollar, "a top secret program created by the Defense Intelligence Agency (DIA) to use whatever tools possible to retrieve Soviet war materiel—mostly the dummy warheads from test launches—from the sea floor." And there, Craven met Jim Bradley, the commanding officer of a Pentagon office whose primary goal was to "find and recover warheads off the seafloor so that engineers could pick apart and construct their guidance system and construction."

Bradley oversaw the repurposing of an obsolete nuclear submarine dubbed the *Halibut* as an oceanographic research vessel. "The sub was given a two-ton aluminum 'fish'—a twelve-foot-long robot outfitted with radar, sonar, cameras and strobe lights that could be deployed from the hatch and towed under the sub on several miles of steel cable, providing Craven a way to photograph the ocean depths." The "Bat Cave," a three-level special intelligence operations space aboard the *Halibut* sported a dark room, data analysis center, and the largest computer installed on board a submarine to date, the Univac 1124.

Craven was already briefed on the K-129 issue, having attended numerous top-secret meetings focusing on SOSUS and AFTAC data, notably including a VIP-only conference at the Naval Observatory in Washington D.C. on Monday, May 20, 1968. Word reached Craven about the latest developments at Pearl Harbor.

Craven's deep-sea tools and related techniques became extremely popular after the May 22, 1968 loss of the USS *Scorpion* and the disappearance of K-129. These two disasters could not be more different from a scientific perspective: The K-129, from all available evidence, seemed to have exploded on the surface of the ocean, while *Scorpion* experienced an unexplained "catastrophic accident." The data clearly pointed to this distinction on how each vessel met its fate, but there was no in-depth explanation.

The fact that a loud bang appeared on the hydrophone readers meant that whatever did happen was significant. Yet Craven also guessed that because there was no second blip in the data, the likelihood was that K-129 sank with hatches open while flooding with water. This meant, or Craven thought, that the sub was likely lying intact on the ocean floor.

Monday, July 15, 1968 found Captain Edward Moore heading for the open sea, scanning the horizon as *Halibut* churned past sailboats and fishing boats around Pearl Harbor. Soon she submerged, even as most of the 15 officers, 123 enlisted men, and 6 technicians wondered exactly where they were going and why. Even so, they went to sea with seventy-five movies, many of them first-run Hollywood hits.

About a week later much of the crew had already guessed that their course was north and west into waters often occupied by Soviet vessels. The technicians in the Bat Cave went to work once *Halibut* entered the five-square-mile zone thought to be K-129's resting place. "First, a search grid was laid out. Acoustic transponders were launched through the bow torpedo tubes at specific intervals. Once a transponder came to rest on the ocean floor, its location was noted using internal guidance and added to a chart."

Over the next two days, the crew aboard *Halibut* plotted and calculated the location of each and every transponder, constructing a detailed map of the search area. The objective: a navigational grid that could signal the location of "the fish" and associated cameras passing within five hundred yards of any specific transponder, even though the water in this area was three miles deep.

Launching the fish took many tedious hours and was conducted with extreme care. After all, a malfunction would mean they'd come all this way for nothing.

Soon an ungainly two-ton device hanging from wires just a few yards above the ocean floor closely examined and photographed underwater hills, thermal vents, and seabed lava flows. So began the second phase of the hunt for K-129.

The submarine usually, but not always, swept the area using a consistent, systematic approach. Maintaining a single, constant depth using (and recording) a variety of search patterns helped ensure that no areas would be missed, despite the fact that coordination among the bridge, ballast control operation, planesman, helmsman, and, finally, the ballast control operator was absolutely essential. Crew members in the Bat Cave did their best, staring at hard-to-analyze side-scan sonar images, hoping to see relevant objects that cameras could examine in greater detail.

The submarine planesman commonly operates the horizontal, wing-like planes on the boat's bow or sail, steering the boat up or down. The days filled with increasing frustration, even as they collected photographs of giant sea slugs, fish with large eyes, and creatures seemingly created for a science fiction film. Seven weeks into the mission, Captain Moore decided they'd had enough—at least for now.

The second mission was marked by fresh-food shortages and at long last success. A photograph technician named Billie Joe Price didn't exactly know what he was supposed to be looking for—because his vague orders required photographing anything that looked unusual, whatever that meant.

My God, Price thought, *was that a submarine conning tower?* Even though this was all being recorded at twenty thousand feet, the "fish strobe light" made for an incredibly clear picture, a picture that left no doubt about what was down there: intact steel and four periscopes extended from a submarine, which also sported a rudder and a ship bell resting on the sea floor.

Price configured the numerous useful photographs into a montage. It revealed that the submarine had broken in half, with the bigger portion lying on its side, and tens if not hundreds of holes and tears were visible all over what was left of the hulk. Of course there were many more photographs that didn't provide any insight at all. Yet what he saw now in the montage of the most valuable photographs prompted him to pick up the phone to call the commander. Unreal as it might seem, even as he rang up the captain's stateroom, he spotted a well-dressed skeleton, replete with quilted pants, boots, and a storm raglan. Price told the captain that they'd found what they were looking for.

Back in Pearl Harbor, the crew and their families soon watched it all. Captain Moore and his executive officer (XO) watched from *Halibut*, as three US Navy guys wearing formal uniforms choc a bloc full of medals followed by two armed guards climbed out of a black limousine and walked toward the submarine. This was the cue for Moore and his XO to walk down the plank and off the submarine. The XO sported a black briefcase locked on his wrist, which the guards took from him before climbing back into the limo for a quick trip back to a nearby airfield. The briefcase was Washington bound, filled with photographs that might well change American history.

Bradley stood over those crystal-clear photographs in his secret Pentagon office, left with the impression that the vessel must be in shallow water. "Bradley could see that two of the sub ballistic missile tubes were empty and that there was substantial damage to the steel hull around them, but one of the R-21s [ballistic nuclear missiles] was clearly still there, standing in its silo, and presenting an incredible opportunity for the United States to get its hands on something that seemed almost unfathomable: a Soviet ICBM [Intercontinental Ballistic Missile]with a nuclear warhead."

Bradley took the photographs straight to his boss, Frederick "Fritz" Harlfinger II, who became director of the ONI less than a month earlier.

While Harlfinger served as director of the DIA, the agency scored a Soviet MiG fighter in Syria, Soviet missiles in Vietnam and Indonesia, and a Soviet plane engine in Germany. Raising K-129 arguably might give Harlfinger the intelligence accomplishment of a lifetime.

This opportunity happening not all that long after the Monday, January 22, 1968 North Korean seizure of the USS *Pueblo* would be sweet revenge, indeed.

"That Monday, the USS *Pueblo*, a spy ship flagged as an environmental research vessel was collecting electronic intelligence just outside North Korean boundary waters." The trouble began when a North Korean sub chaser and three torpedo boats appeared nearby. The Korean ships harassed *Pueblo*, which was only lightly armed, and ultimately opened fire. Korean guns strafed the flying bridge with fifty-seven-millimeter explosive rounds, wounding the captain and two other crewmen. The captain of *Pueblo* quickly developed a two-pronged strategy to address the pending capture of his ship. First, he fully cooperated with direct orders from the captain of the North Korean ship nearby. He followed the other ship toward the North Korean port as slowly as he could without drawing hostility and maybe even artillery fire from his adversary. He did this to give his crew as much time as possible to destroy anything and everything of a sensitive nature on board *Pueblo* that might inform the North Koreans in any material way. His intelligence officers smashed machines and burned documents with abandon, throwing some things overboard when they simply ran out of time.

An American sailor named Duane Hodges died that day when the North Korean sub chaser opened up on *Pueblo* just outside North Korean waters. "Seeing no choice, the captain finally relented and surrendered his ship. The North Koreans boarded, bound and blindfolded the crew then docked at Wonsan, where they paraded the captive crew past a crowd of jeering civilians."

That's why American bitterness over *Pueblo* made this opportunity all the sweeter. Bradley and Harlfinger contacted "the rear admiral in charge of submarine warfare," who agreed that they had to raise the K-129 if at all possible. Yet this mission concerned far more than revenge.

This situation provided a unique opportunity to obtain critical information about Soviet nuclear warheads—far beyond what could be collected and analyzed by measuring missile telemetry (essentially detailed performance and direction) once Soviet missiles left the launch pad. Acquiring a Soviet missile warhead would provide significant opportunities to perform detailed analysis of design, guidance, and defensive systems, not to mention reverse engineering opportunities. American scientists in that place and time had no way to measure the power and lethality of Soviet missiles, much less Soviet missile accuracy. Nor was there any way to gauge how many warheads Soviet submarines carried. Finally, the Americans suspected that the Soviet submarines might carry some detectible but fake "dummy" missiles, which might mislead the Americans about aggregated Soviet missile firepower

The upside for the Americans was startlingly clear. Even better, there was the opportunity to recover the submarine communication system for enciphering and deciphering code, in other words the cryptography.

Naval intelligence analysts coveted the possibility of translating the tons and tons of coded Russian chatter that they were currently intercepting thanks to National Security Agency (NSA) satellites silently circling Earth. Getting their hands on a Russian cryptologic machine would enable naval intelligence to do just that, thanks to the equipment recovered from K-129. Movements, commands, and messages would only be the beginning of what they could see once they had a Russian cryptologic machine.

Not long before the Russian K-129 found its way to the bottom of the ocean, Congress learned from a high-ranking navy admiral that the Soviets now operated a fleet of some 100 missile-firing submarines and another 250 attack submarines, aggregating into the largest submarine fleet anyone in any country ever accumulated. This was no exaggeration, if a purportedly comprehensive survey produced by the American Naval War College in 1969 was correct. Worse still, the Soviet submarine fleet was currently growing at a rate never seen before.

At the time, the Americans could build only ten to twelve nuclear subs a year to face the twenty to thirty nuclear submarines built each year by the Soviets.

Harlfinger pitched the K-129 mission, now called Velvet Fist, to President Lyndon B. Johnson, but the order to proceed came later from President Richard Nixon, at the insistence of the deputy national security adviser. Alexander Haig "wanted the photographs to show Nixon personally." This was a gross violation of security protocol, which required that the photographs never leave the possession of ONI personnel. Still, Bradley and Harlfinger didn't want to lose the opportunity to have Velvet Fist approved, so they gave Haig the photographs for twenty-four hours.

Haig persuaded Nixon to approve the project, but responsibility shifted from the US Navy to the CIA. Carl Duckett, a native of western North

Carolina and recently appointed deputy director of the Directorate of Science and Technology, now had the football.

And Parangosky became the quarterback. The top CIA brass tasked a top-secret task force to recover K-129 on July 1, 1969. But then the lawyers got involved.

Maritime law at that time prohibited one country from salvaging the military equipment of another country. This prohibition covered submarines, but once a sunken military vessel was abandoned, the prohibition no longer applied. The CIA argued that K-129 had been abandoned, because the Russians initially mounted a massive search for the vessel, but soon gave up and never resumed any efforts to find it.

Another legal argument at that time posited an incident some forty years earlier in which the Soviets raised a British submarine the Russian Bolsheviks sank in 1919. After returning the remains of British sailors on the submarine, the Soviets repaired and launched it as a Soviet L-class submarine.

The Project Azorian task force launched on July 1, 1969, headquartered in an undisclosed Tyson's Corner, Virginia location sixteen miles from downtown Washington, soon confronted the underlying problem.

"You can't pick up the goddamn submarine or it will fall apart," Bradley told Duckett when he delivered the CIA's preferred concept. "That's a pipe dream." That said, other navy men were more receptive to this "pipe dream." The chief of naval operations, Thomas H. Moorer, supported the CIA plan and ran that support up the flagpole all the way to defense secretary Melvin Laird, who had his doubts but approved the plan anyway. Laird hoped for success, because the proposed lift system just might help the United States recover some of its own distressed or abandoned subs.

November 1969 found Global Marine and Mechanics Research, Inc., engineers ensconced in the Tishman Building on Century Boulevard near Los Angeles International Airport studying a "green book" containing a dozen or so CIA engineering concepts for raising a submarine off the ocean floor. Crooke, Jimmy Dean, and Jack Reed quickly concluded that most of these concepts were only that. They soon concluded, "The only way for the Agency [CIA] to get that sub up from the bottom [of the ocean]—if such a thing were possible—was by using the 'brute strength' or 'dead lift' method." They would have to pull it up on the end of a string of pipe, the longest and heaviest pipe ever built. More Global Marine engineers s were brought in to help design a massive ship similar to those Global Marine had constructed for deep-sea drilling.

This would be a challenge, because the ship would attract the immediate attention of the Soviet Union, now monitoring the Pacific Ocean ever so closely. Soon Russ Thornburg, then–vice president of Oceanics joined the effort. Thornburg and Crooke pondered how to explain "why a giant ship would be operating at a standstill in a remote area of the Pacific" in a manner that might, just might, fool the Russians.

They gamed the problem for hours. Engine problems or similar excuses might buy them a week at best, setting aside the very real possibility that other ships might come to the rescue and discover the real situation before the submarine could be lifted to the surface—a process that might take months. Thornburg argued that a plausible explanation was staring them in the face.

Mining on the ocean floor was widely being discussed in the marine industry press and in Global Marine plans for the future.

Two years later, in 1970, National Security Adviser Henry Kissinger formally proposed a clandestine effort to recover K-129. Once Nixon approved the plan, CIA efforts to make that happen began. In late 1970, Howard Hughes, owner of Hughes Tool Company, then among the richest men in the world, agreed through representatives negotiating with the CIA to assist in the search for Azorian.

The deal was intriguingly basic. Pursuant to a classified "black" contract with the CIA, Hughes would become a secret proxy for the operation. After the black contract was executed, Hughes Tool would begin hiring specific contractors preselected by the CIA and referred to Hughes. All of these contracts would be publicly attributed to a deep-sea mining operation. One of the first public contracts, if not the very first, would be with Global Marine.

Hughes Tool and the CIA signed a contract to this effect on December 13, 1970.

The money financing these operations would be moved from the CIA to Global Marine via Hughes Tool in transactions so secret that the Global Marine accountants didn't even know who the true customer was.

Global Marine didn't build vessels; it designed them. Crooke strongly recommended that the CIA hire Sun Shipbuilding and Drydock Company in Chester, Pennsylvania, eighteen miles southwest of Philadelphia, to construct Hughes Glomar Explorer. The shipyard established in the late nineteenth century now belonged to the Pew family, who had founded the Sun Oil Company, later known as Sunoco. Due to the nature of the project, only the Sun Oil chairman, Bob Dunlap, knew any details about it. Three shifts worked on the project, directed by twenty-seven-year-old design engineer

Jon Matthews, who worked twelve-hour days six days a week, spending only Sundays with his wife and three children.

~ ~

October 1972
The Sun Shipbuilding flyer mailed to contractors, yard workers, and the media in late October 1972 announced "Family Day" featuring the launch of Hughes Glomar Explorer, constructed for Global Marine.

The area around Sun Hull #661, now rising on the horizon in the ship-yard, would become a party venue from eleven in the morning until one thirty in the afternoon on Saturday, November 4, complete with an arts-and-crafts exhibit, refreshments, balloons for the kiddies, and a tour of the US Navy destroyer USS Lowry anchored nearby. But most important, attendees would witness the official launch of Hughes Glomar Explorer (HGE) at noon.

Then, as now, the launching of the ship didn't mean that all work was complete.

> *The ship that slid down the ramp and into the murky Delaware River was only tack welded meaning it was barely able to float without sinking. At that point, the ship was just a hull, with the inner bottom, wing walls, main engines, generators, tunnel thrusters, shafts, motors and a partial amount of bilge and ballast piping. It had at best 50 percent of the wiring installed, a portion of the fire-main system and some, but not all of the sewage tanks.*

Matthews hoped that the boat would be completed in early 1973.

Thursday, April 12, 1973 brought the first sea trials for Hughes Glomar Explorer. Down the Delaware River she sailed, beneath the steel twin sus-pension Delaware Memorial Bridge, out into the Delaware Bay and beyond, and into the Atlantic. The operation was a smooth one, and the written sea assessments emphasized that "overall seaworthiness, mobility and response [responsiveness] are excellent."

The ship passed all deep-water sea trials with an unusually large number of observers onboard. System propulsion, water purification, sewage treat-ment, and air-conditioning were all tested. "They ran the engines at full speed, then threw them into reverse to determine the distance the ship would travel before coming to a crash stop."

Perhaps the most critical tests focused on whether the ship could maintain a position without drifting in open water—a feature that would be critical in successfully raising the Soviet submarine from the bottom of the ocean. To test this ability the Hughes Glomar Explorer crew "laid a series of transponders on the bottom past the thousandth [sic] fathom line and then fired up the station-keeping system—three bow thrusters, two stern thrusters and a twin-screw propulsion system that, together, could hold the ship still within six feet of a fixed point for twenty-four hours." Mission accomplished.

And yet the most critical tests that ideally should have been performed could not be performed at all, because there was no practical way to replicate raising a distressed, deteriorated, and partially destroyed submarine to the surface. Among other questions that had to be answered was whether the K-129 could be raised to the surface as Hughes Glomar Explorer bucked and rocked in even the most moderately disturbed waters.

The captain looked for the roughest water he could find, and, no, the platform didn't budge despite this challenge. Hughes Glomar Explorer left Chester for Long Beach, California on July 24, 1973, deferring a number of tests for arrival on the West Coast. In order to enhance the cover story and avoid public disclosure of the true mission of the ship, the Sun Shipbuilding public relations man described Hughes Glomar Explorer as "a 36,000 ton experimental mining ship," adding, "Sun's delivery of the vessel brought to a close a new ship construction that was heavily engineering oriented."

The press release highlighted unique characteristics and numerous innovations, going on to say that when it arrived in California, extensive mining equipment manufactured by Lockheed would be installed so that the ship could conduct mining-system and equipment tests in the Pacific Ocean.

The London *Observer* erroneously linked "the ship's intended path, down the coast of Latin America, with a rumor that Howard Hughes' secret partner in the mining venture was Nicaraguan President Anastasio Somoza." The dictator supposedly offered Howard Hughes a tax-free base for his mining operations.

During the first leg of the journey, from Chester to Bermuda, the crew performed some forty-seven different system tests, all of which were uneventful. Hughes Glomar Explorer left Bermuda for Long Beach on August 11, even as much of the crew finished out details, such as installing small components replacing temporary welds with permanent ones and testing smaller systems. The trip down the east coast of South America and into the Pacific was largely uneventful. Hughes Glomar Explorer sailed into Long Beach at five o'clock in the afternoon on September 30, 1973 for a transition from a mining ship to its true purpose: salvaging a Soviet submarine. Crooke fired the entire sea voyage crew upon arrival, because there wasn't any more work for them. A series of metal containers was transported to Long Beach on trucks. The containers included a darkroom for processing film and photographs, a drying compartment, a decontamination container for nuclear material, a morgue for processing any human remains encountered, and even containers for changing clothes. The ship nerve center would be a set of two control vans installed in an empty compartment on the upper deck of the deckhouse, while other vans had been prepared specifically to deal with the recovery of intelligence from K-129. The work was tedious, hot, and often carried out in confined spaces deep in the bowels of the ship during long shifts.

Because only non-union men were hired for the upcoming voyage to salvage K-129, the Marine Engineers Union picketed Hughes Glomar Explorer, telling the press and anyone who would listen how the dismissed crew for the voyage from Chester to Long Beach had received no overtime and were cramped together in small staterooms, contrary to customary practices at that time. The picketers and protesters became increasingly aggressive, harassing the new crew members as they arrived and departed Hughes Glomar Explorer and stopping delivery trucks from time to time. Worse still, two navy men assigned to the mission who were supposed to blend in could not do so. They were often spotted policing the deck by picking up cigarette butts and trash. Finally, one of the CIA men ordered them to loosen up.

Soon came the time to test the capability of the ship to perform the work for which it was designed and constructed, namely to lift an entire submarine from the bottom of the ocean through gates in the bottom of the ship without anyone on the surface of the ocean knowing what was going on. A "capture vehicle" much like a claw would be lowered from the ship on a pipe string, similar to those used on drilling rigs to drill for oil, to snag the submarine and pull it inside the bottom of the ship. The capture vehicle was nicknamed Clementine for reasons that remain unclear to this day.

The first tests of the pipe handling system (PHS) and heavy-lift system in January 1974 were hardly successful. Despite this and other setbacks, the PHS issue and other problems were sufficiently resolved for a June 20, 1974 departure from Long Beach, under the command of Mission Director Dale Nielsen. Hughes Glomar Explorer arrived at the target site on July 4, and the search began.

Hughes Glomar Explorer carried a huge "black" box containing an early rudimentary satellite navigation system that the crew could use one or two times a day, but only when satellites were directly overhead. That said, Hughes Glomar Explorer was hard to miss. The British cargo ship *Bel Hudson* called on July 13 asking for assistance with a sailor who had sustained a heart attack. Five days later the bulky, 459-foot Soviet missile ship *Chazmha* hove into view, quickly launching a helicopter to circle Hughes Glomar Explorer for ten minutes or so. When asked by a *Chazmha* radio operator what Hughes Glomar Explorer was up to, the response was brief to say the least.

"We are conducting ocean-mining tests."

The *Chazmha* radio operator wished his counterpart aboard Hughes Glomar Explorer luck, and the Russians departed at nine that evening. The *Chazmha* commanding officer, Captain Krasnov, wired his superiors that from all appearances Hughes Glomar Explorer was conducting mining operations, just as the Americans had told him.

Clementine went into water just before midnight on Sunday, July 21. "The weather was calm and the sea as flat as it had been in days, but a pesky four-foot swell was rocking the ship from side to side. Conditions weren't ideal, but with a month gone and severe weather on the way, this was as good as it was going to get. It was clear to everyone on board by this point that there was never going to be a perfect moment. Even as the first two sections of pipe to go down had to be pulled up and readjusted, a blip on the radar screen several miles away showed another vessel approaching the Explorer."

In for a penny, in for a pound. Not knowing whether the approaching visitors were friends or enemies, the crew continued the operation. Curiously enough, the approaching visitor peeled off and disappeared, only to return just before eleven o'clock in the morning. The Americans could see "this was a tiny ship relative to the Explorer—a 155-foot tug identified by the eyes and ears in the sky as the SB-10, an allegedly civilian salvage vessel of a type widely used by the Soviets as undercover intelligence ships. Often, these tugs accompanied submarines on patrol and carried divers."

Before long the two vessels came so close to each other that the crews could easily see what their counterparts were up to. The Americans couldn't help but notice that a few Soviet crew members were wearing swimming suits, although most were in standard fatigues. There was even a woman on board the Soviet vessel. The Russian crew members took extensive photographs of Hughes Glomar Explorer, whether for their own entertainment or official purposes. Some of the equipment aboard Hughes Glomar Explorer broke down during this "cultural exchange." That said, the Americans were undeterred in their mission, laying down some ten thousand feet of pipe by noon Thursday, even as the SB-10 sailed as close as 100 feet away from Hughes Glomar Explorer at great risk due to the heavy fog in the area, all for the purpose of harassing the American crew.

The crew on Hughes Glomar Explorer couldn't know that "satellites were intercepting every message the tug sent and bouncing those messages directly to Washington, where NSA analysts listened and then passed word to the CIA that there was nothing to worry about."

Still, the dangerously close Soviet surveillance and photography persisted, leaving the Americans wondering if things were going to get worse. "What if they [the Soviets] boarded with weapons? No one had a really good answer." Or so it seemed. "Very few people knew of the guns that the security staff had stashed under" a bunk. The crew had been told not to worry about this, but rumors on board Hughes Glomar Explorer persisted. One fable told of a navy submarine shadowing Hughes Glomar Explorer, too far away for the Soviet tug to notice her, but close enough to rescue the Americans if it came to that.

The actual procedures to be followed should the Soviet tug become overly aggressive were quite clear. "The first step would be to advise a Soviet vessel to stand down and not board. If that was ignored, the ship would issue an open distress signal to Naval Command that the mining ship Hughes Glomar Explorer was being boarded by men with guns from a vessel claiming to be a Soviet ship." Truth be told, the Americans didn't know what to expect were the situation to come to that.

The crew focused on the task before them: dropping Clementine to the bottom of the ocean and lifting several million pounds of submarine to the surface. As the capture vehicle approached the bottom, the sonar aboard Clementine captured "an irregular hump" across what had been a flat line seconds before. That irregular hump was no other than the K-129. On the surface above, practically everyone on board Hughes Glomar Explorer came to the control room for a quick look at the K-129 before access was limited to those who worked there.

Clementine hovered over the wreck, as camera operators tried to ignore the surrounding sea life of huge, blind fish swimming in and out of camera view, strange-looking crabs, and God knows what else. Following a few minutes' observation, they began positioning their tripod-mounted cameras to maximize their chances of finding anything about the position of the submarine on the ocean floor, the overall condition of the hull, or obstructions on the sea floor that could complicate the operation by snagging the claw.

Hughes Glomar Explorer creaked and groaned with the weight of some twelve million pounds hanging from the derrick on the deck—and this was before Clementine grasped K-129 into its claws for the slow trip up into the hands of the Americans. Once Clementine was close enough to grab the sub, the American engineers aboard Hughes Glomar Explorer began discussing, or some would say arguing, about whether to gently grasp or firmly grab K-129 for the trip up. In the end the Americans decided to gently slide around the submarine and carefully bring it to the surface, for fear that a firm grasp would damage the hull. The lift out would be slow, to minimize the changes of damaging the entire lift system. And so they began.

There wasn't a place on the retrieval ship where crew members couldn't hear the noise emanating from the sea bottom where the lifting system pulled and strained, making slow progress clawing at the submarine and dragging the wreck up toward the ocean surface. Pistons pushed, pipes pulled, and somehow the straining system got the wrecked up into the waves beneath a clear sky. This brought cheers, of course, but only for a few minutes, because the entire crew sighed together at the very thought of getting the 16,500 feet of pipe up as well. Naturally something broke in the middle of all this effort. Such events were to be expected while struggling through such a massive job. And now the "heavy-compensation system broke down, delaying everybody and everything associated with the mission—if only for a few hours." This must have seemed bizarre to the crew, who could glance periodically at the submarine—or what was left of it—hanging in Clementine's claw as frantic efforts to fix the pump seemed to go on forever.

Still, Nielsen was confident enough to begin preparing for the next phase of the operation.

The principles developed a basic cover story for this next phase, which would involve either Midway Island or Lahaina, Hawaii before the operation even began. The focus would be on Midway, which as a naval base was best equipped to facilitate what had to be done next, even though a cover story was required. Nielsen announced to the world over open radio channels that a "nodule collector vehicle" had been damaged. This supposedly happened when the vehicle struck a silt-covered outcrop. Nielsen asked for permission to proceed into the navy facilities at Midway.

A fake Midway assessment of the fake damage would justify sending the ship to the US mainland, where the "repairs" could be performed. In fact CIA officers sent to Midway would unload the critical assets extracted during the operation—specifically missiles and code books for undocumented extraction in the dark—freeing Hughes Glomar Explorer to continue with the less important elements of the mission while returning to the United States.

This was not to say that things were quiet on Hughes Glomar Explorer. For those men on the heavy-lift and pipe-handling crews, the slow process of raising Clementine and her target back to the surface was anything but boring. Every moment was tense. Worse still, "As the sub rose, one-inch diameter steel bolts began to strain and hiss and eventually pop loose, firing across the deck like bullets." And that was before the crew realized, at about nine o'clock on the morning of August 4, that suddenly and without expectation, the submarine being lifted to the surface lost much weight. "Whatever happened was sudden and violent," one crew member told another. Even though the video feed focused on K-129 showed no change, someone quickly realized that the camera was set to update the live feed only when some change within the camera frame occurred. Now they realized that outside the camera frame at least half the submarine had fallen back into the sea. All they could do was hope that the most important contents, the missiles that had brought the crew all this way at the cost of millions of dollars, remained in the grasp of Clementine. When CIA officials at Langley, Virginia were notified, they suggested, for reasons that remain unclear, that the part of the submarine still in Clementine's grasp be dropped so that the mission could be started afresh.

Even after CIA leadership at Langley learned that Clementine had been damaged, the crew was ordered one more time to start all over again, until at last reason prevailed. On the evening of Tuesday, August 6, the Russian SB-10 trawler made one more pass near Hughes Glomar Explorer. The entire crew exposed their pale Russian butts to Hughes Glomar Explorer's crew, some of whom returned the favor. And with that, the Russian trawler horn blasted three times before sailing back to Russia, not knowing how close K-129 was to the surface that very moment.

Three days later, on Friday, August 9, 1974, the recovery of K-129 was complete, even as Nixon turned in his resignation and left the White House, murmuring to the very last that he was not a crook. Newly minted president Gerald Ford learned about the limited success of the Hughes Glomar Explorer the very next day, just as news stories about the mission began to appear in the world press. A few days later the crew learned that

John Graham, the chief Global Marine naval architect who had designed Hughes Glomar Explorer, had died. His last wish was that his ashes be scattered from the deck of Hughes Glomar Explorer, and that was accomplished, legal or not.

The bodies of the six Soviet sailors who had been recovered during the operation were buried at sea with full military honors on September 4. Hughes Glomar Explorer sailed into Long Beach during the early morning hours of Saturday, September 21 so that the Soviet missiles and other critical contents of K-129 could be unloaded in the darkness. Although the 26 million dollar mission was deemed a success, critics derailed the 36 million dollar follow-up effort to recover the rest of K-129, despite the personal support of Kissinger. One source later claimed that in December 1974 a Soviet navy officer warned a counterpart in the US Navy that a mission to recover the rest of K-129 would have meant war.

Eventually, perhaps inevitably, the *Los Angeles Times* and *New York Times* ran stories about the raising of K-129, but both publishers buried the story in back pages. The *Washington Post*, *Newsweek*, and *Time* all ran "back-page" stories as well, after listening to anguished pleas from the CIA director. Eventually investigative reporter Jack Anderson turned the raising of K-129 into a front-page story.

Published reports suggest that for reasons that remain murky, the CIA considers Project Azorian, in which at least two Soviet nuclear torpedoes were recovered, to be one of the greatest intelligence coups of the Cold War.

CHAPTER 9

Fearless Resolve

Robert Lewis (Bob) Howard lay in the dirt a long way from, Opelika, the county seat of Lee County on the eastern border of Alabama, the place he called home. Opelika is Creek for "large swamp," and in a sense Howard was still in a swamp, surrounded as he was by north Vietnamese regulars, looking around at what was left of his thirty-two-man reconnaissance (recon) team. Tomorrow would be the last day of 1968, and Howard might have wondered whether he would see it arrive. The North Vietnamese Army (NVA) infantry was all around him, firing into the dense jungle at anything and everything that moved. The first lieutenant who led them into this place as platoon commander was stretched out on the ground nearby, his body shredded from head to toe by bullets and grenade fragments. Four South Vietnamese regulars were also in the dirt—one was already dead, and the rest yelled and screamed in agony.

Square jawed, tall, powerfully built, but quiet, shy, and unassuming, had he been in civilian clothing, few would ever guess that Howard earned a Distinguished Service Cross and a Silver Star, based on two separate nominations for the Medal of Honor. Fewer still would guess that he'd overcome poverty and God knows what else to become an honored warrior.

And yet he had, but now he paid the price. The grenade had knocked him down, cutting into his head. The blood was everywhere, covering his hands, groin, legs, and feet. Dragging himself up from the ground, he couldn't help but see the guy with a flamethrower—and it wasn't made in Chicago. The North Vietnamese soldier was moving around among wounded and dead

Americans brandishing his weapon, using it to finish off some men and simply to roast the others. God, what would the grandmother who raised him back in Alabama think of this?

So it went, not in South Vietnam but in Cambodia, beyond the reach of any Americans that might have helped Howard escape from this grisly spectacle. Because this was a super dark covert operation, if asked, the American government would deny that Moore and his men were even conducting this operation, much less send in the cavalry to rescue them.

The North Vietnamese grenade had blown his automatic weapon to hell, taking most of his web gear with it. Howard heard screaming coming from somewhere, wiped the blood from his eyes, and only then could see his second lieutenant yelling out in pain at no one in particular, maybe not even seeing the North Vietnamese soldier looming to his immediate right. Howard had to do something. Somehow his fingers found a single M33 hand grenade still strapped to his side. Despite the new shrapnel wounds, he worked the grenade pin loose.

That's when the NVA regular saw Howard and turned the flamethrower in his direction. "In the midst of rising smoke, rattling gunfire and the screams of dying men, Howard and his opponent made direct eye contact. The American felt his enemy was experiencing a smug sense of satisfaction knowing he was about to burn a Green Beret to death."

So Stephen L. Moore describes one of many life-threatening encounters experienced by Howard in Moore's account of the "Studies and Observation Group" in *Uncommon Valor: The Recon Company That Earned Five Medals of Honor and Included America's Most Decorated Green Beret*, the 2018 book that served as a primary source for quotations for this chapter. Howard, then a sergeant, worked out of Special Forces Forward Operating Base No. 2 (FOB-2) near Kontum in the Central Highlands of South Vietnam.

The Studies and Observation Group (SOG) directed by the Military Assistance Command, Vietnam (MACV), a unit comprised of volunteers from the Army Green Berets, a smattering of Navy SEALs (Sea, Air, and Land), and even a few CIA operatives, not to mention some indigenous staff members, used this advanced base as a recon company operations center.

The MACV created the SOG in 1964 to work along the Ho Chi Minh trail, massively defended though it was, to find bombing mission targets, perform strategic reconnaissance, sabotage enemy ammunition and other facilities, obtain intelligence by capturing enemy soldiers, and other means. SOG secrecy was so strict that the American government denied the very existence of SOG, even as its men undertook the most perilous of assignments in South Vietnam, Laos, and Cambodia.

Beyond that, the SOG warriors also saved a number of downed American pilots from death or imprisonment during "Bright Light" missions operating deep in enemy country.

Usually these Green Berets assigned to the SOG dropped into enemy territory from helicopters in small reconnaissance groups of two or three, often with a like number of indigenous soldiers from the insertion area, wearing uniforms entirely devoid of any American insignia. These American soldiers didn't even carry weapons made in the United States. Like the characters in the then-contemporary television series "Mission Impossible," the secretary of the army would disavow any knowledge of their mission should they be killed or captured. Yet these SOG Green Berets conducted operations that were highly effective. Some sources claim that in 1969 these operators had the highest kill ratio of any American unit in the Vietnam War—a mortality ratio between the number of North Vietnamese regulars killed and each lost Green Beret of 150 to 1.

Quite often the SOGs were tracked by NVA regulars from the very moment the helicopters inserted them into enemy territory—more often than not the jungle. "They remained on the ground for days or even for more than a week at a time with meager rations and only the ammunition each man could carry, often engaging platoon-to-division-sized enemy forces until the surviving members could be extracted by helicopter. Sometimes, entire teams were wiped out." According to John Plaster, whose 1997 book, *SOG: The Secret Wars of America's Commandos in Vietnam*, served as another source for this chapter, the recon company at FOB-2 Kontum, whose members included Howard, was the most decorated unit of the Vietnam War, with five Medal of Honor recipients honored between February 1967 and January 1970. During that same period, FOB-2 recon men received eight Distinguished Service Crosses, not to mention numerous Purple Hearts. Many of the missions these men performed remain highly classified and unknown to this day.

Howard hid his fierce courage beneath the frequent silence of a modest man living out a proud military heritage. That tradition was handed down by a great-grandfather who died in action during World War I, not to mention a father and two uncles killed as World War II paratroopers a few years after Howard was born in mid-July 1939.

Life was tough in Opelika during World War II. Howard and his sisters picked cotton to help his extended family survive. Howard remembered that despite their poverty, his grandmother shipped homemade cookies to the troops serving in foreign lands. He finished high school in June 1956 and immediately enlisted in the army, despite being a star football player who very well might have received an athletic scholarship to college in Alabama or elsewhere.

Years later he remembered the details of the basic training he received in the army. They trained with wooden weapons until real ones became available. "And then when they finally issued our M1 rifles, they only gave us three rounds of ammunition to zero our weapons." There was little doubt about the path Howard would follow if he had the chance after basic training. He would earn paratrooper wings like his father and uncles before him.

Nine years later Howard traveled to Vietnam for his first tour as a member of the 101st Airborne Division. While recovering in hospital from a rifle bullet that ricocheted during one of his first missions into his face from a tree, Howard was recruited to join Special Forces. He arrived at Kontum late in the spring of 1967 and went on his first mission that summer.

His first action came that summer when two Vietcong snipers tried to take Howard and a supply sergeant out after a broken-down truck left them stranded on a makeshift bridge. Within minutes the snipers were dead. Despite his day job as a supply sergeant, Howard begged his way onto several combat missions as an extra hand. Such volunteers were called "straphangars" for reasons that remain unclear. During the months that followed, FOB-2 commanders nominated Howard three times for a Medal of Honor. Number three was the charm.

He tagged along with Sergeant First Class Johnnie Gilreath and Sergeant Larry Williams on a November 19, 1968, ST (Spike Team) Colorado mission into southeast Laos. While looking for water to replenish what they had carried in their canteens, Williams had discovered a large cache of rice near a stream undoubtedly left there for NVA regulars. After calling for helicopters to insert more men, designated the Hatchet Force, to help destroy the huge rice supply, Williams, Gilreath, Howard, and the others encountered a single NVA regular and then at least four others. Howard gunned down the enemy quartet even as more NVA regulars arrived on the scene.

"All hell broke loose," Williams later remembered. The brown wet stuff hit the fan. Three helicopters carrying Hatchet Force reinforcements limped into their target landing zones as the original mission men worked feverishly destroying rice, salt, and pillboxes. Beneath the mounds of food supplies, they found an estimated thousand rounds of recoilless rifle rounds, not to mention about seven hundred AK47 bullets. While all this was going on, Gilreath watched Howard run toward the enemy every time the enemy showed his face.

Seconds after taking out the immediate threat of four NVA regulars, Howard and his men dug even deeper into the dirt at the sound of new machine-gun fire coming from yet another NVA emplacement. Howard instinctively knew what had to be done and began the long, dangerous crawl toward the NVA nest, killing one enemy sniper along the way before taking out an entire NVA machine-gun nest with point-blank M16 rifle fire.

And still there was danger. The unmistakable sound of more fire from yet another nest roared into action, forcing Howard to move the American unit back into a place where the machine gun couldn't hurt them as he called in an air strike to settle the NVA hash. Minutes later, Howard low crawled into position to assess the damage himself, only to discover the hard way that the NVA regulars were still alive. He dug in deep enough to keep the machine-gun fire six inches above his head, pulled out a grenade, and took out the nest, if only for a few minutes.

Running for all he was worth, Howard got back to the platoon just in time to see yet another NVA cluster drop into the machine-gun nest. He had just enough time to put his hands on an anti-tank rocket launcher and aim it at the enemy just as the enemy weapon roared into life. This sent rounds buzzing around his head just before the American rocket ended this problem permanently, giving Howard plenty of time to move his platoon to safety, however temporary.

Now the Americans realized they had stumbled upon a large logistical supply area surrounded by at least an NVA battalion operating out of an extensive bunker system. Amazingly, the only American casualty in this encounter was Howard himself. After all Americans were out of the area, air strikes were called in against the NVA position. Howard was nominated for the Medal of Honor, but in time the army awards board downgraded the commendation to the Distinguished Service Cross, the second-highest American award for valor.

Three weeks later Howard left the supply room again for yet another recon operation with Sergeant Larry Williams and Spike Team (ST) Colorado for a December 7 long-range patrol. Their mission was to recon an NVA battalion headquarters and supply area that Howard and the others had discovered, calling in air strikes on NVA troops they encountered en route. The next day, on December 10, they discovered yet another enemy camp, this one housing a complete battalion in some twenty-one battalion structures, all of which Howard and other team members destroyed, along with twenty tons of rice, a ton of medical supplies, and thousands of pounds of guns and ammunitions.

Soon, thirty to fifty NVA regulars struck ST Colorado as Howard searched for an extraction landing zone (LZ). Williams quickly got on the radio to beg for aerial support before moving most of his group toward the landing zone area selected; Howard and his team held off the NVA. Huey helicopters extracted them.

Eventually, Howard would be awarded the Bronze Star with V device for leading the effort to destroy the enemy supplies and for continually exposing himself to enemy fire while his team was being extracted. Awards meant little to him, but it was the fearless resolve of men like Howard that had helped SOG teams complete ninety-seven missions into Cambodia by late 1967.

But then, in the early morning hours of January 31, 1968, the Vietnamese New Year, the NVA launched the Tet Offensive. That brought a long-range recon mission for ST Colorado and a tag-along opportunity beside Williams and Paul Poole for Howard, who was more than welcome. February 1, the last day of the mission, brought an aggressive attack by a large NVA unit that quickly pinned down Howard, Williams, Poole, and the rest of the men with massive automatic weapons fire.

Howard practically dared the NVA to shoot him while moving his Vietnamese troops into the most effective firing positions possible, multi-tasking by killing a large number of NVA as he moved along. Poole, in the meantime, begged for air support, not to mention an emergency extraction. Now came the time for Howard to cover the rest of the men as they ran and jumped into a deep bomb crater for shelter from incoming fire while they waited for American air support.

Howard did nothing to promote any reward for himself, but higher command recognized his efforts by proposing him for awards whenever merited.

Later, Howard and Poole would be awarded the Army Commendation for heroism for their actions during those early days of the Tet Offensive. Yet two weeks into that offensive, and from time to time thereafter, the hottest area of operation for SOG teams was a region known as "the Bra," a geographic feature on the Dak Xou River consisting of double bends resembling a woman's brassiere, easily spotted from an airplane or helicopter. Highway

110 ran along the river at this point as it snaked its way back into the Central Highlands of South Vietnam near Northern Cambodia. At one of the bends of the Bra, Highway 110 split northeastward from the Ho Chi Minh Trail's major north-south route, Highway 96. This area was heavily defended by the NVA and contained some of the deadliest Kontum target locations—Hotel 9, India-9, Juliet-9, November-9, and Quebec-1. The NVA base known as Binh Tram 37 was a major stockpile of weapons and supplies defended by massed antiaircraft guns and counter-recon units was also hidden in the Bra.

March 1968 found Howard, the supply sergeant who was always looking for action, joining various teams for any mission that needed an experienced hand. That month he became an assistant team leader for his old friend Poole and ST Colorado, a unit now designated RT Colorado.

Saturday, March 30, 1968 brought Poole and his small unit into direct contact with yet another massive group of NVA regulars making its way down a hill. Poole spotted them just in time to send his unit racing off for protection while he darted back and forth through AK-47 rounds to plant a Claymore mine where the NVA troops would never expect it. Staying close enough to detonate the device when it would maximize NVA fatalities, he killed eight and managed to escape with only a minor hand injury.

Now Poole himself went out on the point, moving ahead of head men down a ravine toward a landing zone, taking two hits from NVA regulars. At about the same time, Howard added yet another Purple Heart to his chest just before a defective rifle grenade fell between two of his team members, even as they all ran for their lives.

One of Howard's favorite tricks while being chased by NVA regulars—if and only if he had time—was to remove his often sweat-stained and sometimes bloody shirt and find a small tree or bush to hang it over near the path the NVA regulars were likely to take. And right in front of this decoy he would scatter and then hide several "toe poppers"—small M-14 anti-personnel mines for which V40 mini-fragmentation anti-personnel mines were substituted. Usually but not always the NVA regulars would stop long enough to get a close look at the shirt and detonate a mine or two, losing a man or two doing so. While Howard was doing this, Poole took a position just shy of the landing zone, using his M79 grenade launcher to keep the NVA regulars at bay while radio man Charles Dunlap radioed in the choppers.

Later Poole received a Silver Star for his gallantry in this action, but jewelry was the furthest thing from his mind that day.

Two weeks after sustaining yet another set of injuries, Howard became a platoon adviser working with Captain Gene McFarley. His lunch with a Hatchet Force company of native troops on Tuesday, April 16 was rudely interrupted by a larger NVA unit opening fire. That sent most of the younger native troops rushing up a nearby mountain, joined by McFarley's more seasoned Montagnard tribe comrades.

McFarley ran up the hill as quickly as he could, stopping from time to time to lay down fire and gather his men around him. At the same time, Howard placed his Montagnards into the best defensive posture he could create with NVA fire falling everywhere.

Flying shrapnel and automatic-weapons fire seemed to follow Howard everywhere as he maneuvered into a spot where he could wipe out a crew of NVA regulars serving as a mortar team. McFarley, in the meantime, somehow managed to round up the panicked Montagnards. Thanks to the efforts of former Hatchet Force recon man First Lieutenant Ken Etheredge, a series of air strikes saved the day. During the quiet days that followed, McFarley wrote up Howard, this time for an Army Commendation Medal, citing his heroism in the almost-doomed operation.

Mid-November 1968 once again found Howard out of the supply room. This time he was on patrol with the SLAM (Search, Locate, Annihilate, Monitor) Company pursuing NVA regulars. On the evening of November 15, Howard and his buddies were getting ready for a night's sleep, or so they had hoped, on a small hilltop as their Montagnard allies began digging foxholes. At about four o'clock the following morning, mortar rounds and rifle grenades exploded all around them.

Lieutenant Lee Swain just happened to remember it was his birthday as he aimed his weapon down the hillside, doing what had to be done to survive the day, despite the shrapnel that seemed to be landing everywhere, destroying equipment, clothing, and, all too often, body parts.

Howard and two other men began the long and dangerous crawl toward a rotten tree stump and fallen log nearby, which provided the only cover of any kind to be had. Everyone but Howard was struck by red-hot shrapnel. One of the men, injured though he was, crawled from position to position directing the Montagnards to use only their M79 grenade launchers in order to avoid muzzle flashes, which would give the NVA ready targets. They raised headquarters on the radio and reported the heavy RPG (rocket propelled grenade) attack underway.

The CBU (cluster bomb unit) bomblets, which everyone called "cluster bombs," dropped by Skyraider pilots on Saturday, November 16, 1968, pounded NVA regulars surrounding a SLAM Company position, saving the day once again, even though some eleven men had been severely wounded earlier.

And that's exactly what the company commander asked for, only to be directed to break through the NVA regulars and press on—orders easy enough to give from the safety of a tent at headquarters. Several more requests to have Slam Company extracted were rejected with vigor. The military problem the Americans faced was all too obvious. The company was far too large to go unnoticed. Lieutenant Tom Jaeger was in charge.

Somehow the NVA regulars discovered exactly where the Hatchet Force company camped every night as the Americans weaved and bobbed down Highway 96 toward the suspected location of the NVA 37 mm guns. The lieutenant in charge after his commanding officer departed discovered this predicament all too soon.

Their next RON (remain overnight) site was in a deep jungle so rocky that the men could not dig sleeping depressions. Jaeger asked to be resupplied on the morning of November 17. But they could only watch helplessly as their supplies drifted into the hands of their NVA opponents on a tree line, almost as if by design.

Although these deliveries were not worth the risk of having someone killed or wounded retrieving them, as it happened, one of the two bundles dropped only about one hundred yards from the Americans was fairly easy to bring in. Better yet, the box labeled "mortar ammunition" was full of cigarettes, then in very short supply.

This only whetted the appetite for more stuff, so the entire crew called for food and water to be dropped by chopper in a clearing just about a quarter mile away. They needed to move anyway to minimize their exposure. While doing just that, Howard and a medic named Parnar encountered yet another NVA who had injured one of the Montagnards. Firing as quickly as they could, Howard and Parnar moved the Montagnard to safety.

That's when the Americans were confronted with small arms fire from at least two squads of NVA regulars sweeping over them. The skirmish continued, but the Americans survived, killing at least three Vietcong and wounding several others, forcing the aggressors to move away from the scene of the action. Before this confrontation, Lieutenant Walter Huczko had moved his platoon back to the landing zone where they had started. Despite winning this skirmish, the Americans still could have been attacked in the darkness, if the enemy had been able to discover their exact position. This prompted Parnar to quiet the wounded Montagnard by administering a heavy dose of morphine.

The rest of the night passed peacefully enough, allowing an extraction of the wounded Montagnard on the morning of Monday, November 18. Now the company divided into two columns about sixteen yards apart, moving toward their target area in a configuration allowing them to maximize firepower on either the right or left flank, if needed.

Mid-afternoon found SLAM Company coming out of deep jungle near an intersection between national Highway 96 and a primitive road near a large clearing. Now they were supposed to move toward the clearing, even as the lieutenant ordered in air cover. They arrived there with no opposition.

When Jaeger called out for the company to keep moving, Howard and Swain moved in front of everyone else and carefully moved across a large clearing in the cover of very tall grass. A number of Montagnards spread out in rows on the flanks to repel an attack, should one come.

That's when Howard spotted trouble ahead and asked Swain what they should do. Swain decided they'd better ambush the NVA before they themselves were ambushed. They began firing their CAR-15s on automatic, drawing overwhelming return fire, not to mention rifle grenades. The response affirmed that the American company had almost walked right into a massive NVA kill zone.

Within seconds Jaeger found himself in the center of a firestorm.

They spotted ground fire coming from a nearby tree line, ducked behind the nearest bush, and sprayed the NVA regulars down as quickly as they could. Even so, Swain was injured by an incoming RPG, which pushed his left foot into an ugly twist. He could only guess whether he was going to lose it.

Howard knew immediately that Swain was in bad shape, so bad that he might die before he could be evacuated, if such an evacuation were even possible. His right calf had been blown away by gunfire, and what was left of his leg had been snapped.

Swain now realized that the RPG had taken every part of his leg but the Achilles tendon. He also instinctively knew that if Howard tried to stand them both up, this tall grass was the last thing either one of them would ever see.

Nearby Jaeger was on the radio begging for air support. But he soon dropped the handset and ran through NVA bullets to help a Vietnamese soldier wounded about twenty yards away. While giving the man first aid, he heard someone on the radio say that Swain was injured.

More men came to Swain's aid as a medic gave him morphine for the pain. The NVA began massing to the south, east, and west of the American's position. Because the bulk of the NVA force positioned itself to the south, Jaeger called in heavy ordnance so close that some of it hit the American's position.

Now they could hear the trees above them losing both small and large branches as bomb cluster fragments began dropping down on them. As they administered first aid to Swain, Parnar and Howard were struck by incoming explosives. Parnar was so focused on Swain's injuries that he tried to brush off a burning cluster fragment embedded in his right calf muscle.

That's when a Montagnard cried out for a medic as blood poured from his head wound. Wounded Americans seemed to be everywhere. Just about then Sergeant Lee Dickerson, lying in a bamboo grove, realized that he'd been blinded.

About an hour and a half later, a medevac chopper came into view, even as heavy enemy fire continued to pound Jaeger's SLAM Company. Sergeant Lloyd Gerald O'Daniel became so irritated at a four-man NVA machine-gun crew that had his platoon had pinned down that he grabbed a light antitank weapon, ran as fast as he could toward their emplacement, and killed them all.

Every American there must have wondered whether the medevac choppers could land soon enough to save the seriously wounded. Twenty-year-old Warrant Officer Carl M. Hoeck, the senior pilot leading the flight of four Huey Gladiators, hovered with his team at nine thousand feet a few miles southeast of the battle, while Mike Bingo (yes Bingo) code-named "Cheetah," sorted out the situation from a Cessna 0-2 Skymaster circling nearby. Hoeck learned that several severely wounded men were not likely to survive unless they were picked up soon. He volunteered to go in first, pretending to leave the area and then coming back at low altitude while the rest of the choppers waited some distance away.

After the fake retreat, "Hoeck slowly lowered his collective pitch, added an excessive amount of left pedal and rolled into a tight descending left spiral. The jungle flashed by as cheetah called out headings for the Huey pilot. Suddenly, the jungle thinned into an open area even as Hoeck and his crew began hearing AK small-arms fire and opened up with M60s." This was getting serious.

On his first run past the LZ, Hoeck quickly slouched down into his chicken plate (sliding chest armor) to maximize his cover as his gunners poured nearly all the ammunition they had into the target. During his second run, one of his men spotted an NVA tank 110 yards away, but the tank wasn't the problem.

"As the chopper settled into a hover, a .51-caliber antiaircraft gun on tracks suddenly commenced firing. On the ground Bob Howard suspected it was a half-tracked vehicle he had heard rumbling in the nearby cover." Above Howard, Hoeck "felt rounds slamming into his chopper's right side like someone pounding away with a sledgehammer . . . As his Huey drifted laterally away from the impacting rounds, Hoeck's master caution light was flashing and a glance at the caution panel showed he had lost his engine, hydraulics and everything vital to remaining airborne."

Hoeck knew in a flash that this was it—the ship was dead. He yelled as loud as he could, warning everyone on board that the chopper was going down. He did everything he could to stay in the air long enough to bounce into a thinner patch of jungle than the rough ground all around him. He had to pull to full pitch as he tried to hit the target for minimum bounce.

And then they hit the ground.

The crash-landing bumped Gladiator 167 and everyone inside at least ten feet up into the air, knocking Hoeck into the window just above him. It took everything he had left in him to keep his chopper stable in the dustup of grass and dirt as it went into the ground a second time.

Nearby Jaeger could see a horde of NVA soldiers moving toward the downed helicopter some seventy-five feet away. He didn't think twice—with Howard and several others he jumped up and ran toward Gladiator 167, shooting down NVA regulars as they noticed that the helicopter was now in flames. The entire helicopter crew made it out of the burning wreckage, except Wayne Gilmore, the door gunner. Jaeger and Hoeck got to Gilmore in time to help him out of the chopper, even though he could barely walk. Somehow the entire helicopter crew found the SLAM Company perimeter, even as the ammunition on Gladiator 167 began cooking off in the growing flames.

Any hope of immediate rescue flew away with the remaining rescue helicopters, which were running out of fuel. Only Gladiator 26, piloted by First Lieutenant Craig Collier, remained in the area. "His Gladiator 26 was deep in Laos, low on fuel, and without any gun support. Once the A-1s laid down another round of ordnance against the NVA, Collier figured he would make one final extraction attempt before his fuel was exhausted. He "eased his Huey down on the LZ under fire. The Green Berets knew that every second counted, and they moved to load the most seriously wounded on board Gladiator 26," just as dusk began setting in.

Swain's foot, attached only by the Achilles tendon, dangled out the helicopter door as Gladiator 26 achieved altitude and burned the very last fuel on board reaching Đak Tô . Back at the landing zone, Howard and the rest of the Americans left behind no doubt wondered whether they would get out of this place alive.

Darkness descended on the Americans, as Howard and Jaeger moved from man to man assessing how much ammunition was on hand. Even as the Montagnards dug furiously to create an oval perimeter, Jaeger knew that they needed more ammunition if they were to survive the night, and they begged for it. And arrive it did, forty-five minutes after the ammunition was promised, prompting the NVA to take the initiative.

All too soon, Howard heard the antiaircraft being moved around in the jungle.

Jaeger had to make a big decision quickly if American lives were to be saved. Problem was that his own company of men was likely to pay the price. Their odds of surviving the night in front of them against the NVA were very low, even if they were to get the supplies they needed before darkness. And getting those supplies would be highly risky for the helicopter crew assigned to make an ammunition drop in plain sight of the NVA antiaircraft gun crew that was close by. In the end the decision was easy: Jaeger radioed the ammunition helicopter to turn around and return to base.

Jaeger's men dug in for the night and prepared to make their last stand. Many lay on their backs on the rear edges of their foxholes, hoping that the NVA would not initiate an overnight assault. Jets swept in all around them, dropping all they had before their jet engines faded into the night, only to be replaced by yet another welcome air-support group.

Finally, a Douglas AC-47 "Spooky" gunship nicknamed "Puff the Magic Dragon" brought in the heavy firepower this situation called for. "Three 7.62-mm mini-guns could selectively fire either fifty or a hundred rounds per second. Jaeger had his company outline their perimeter with strobe lights to avoid being hit." Parnar described the moment with precision, recalling that

"The shredding of leaves from the mini-gun rounds ripping through the trees sounded like a summer hailstorm in a forest."

Jaeger began to worry that the same perimeter markings he just ordered to protect his men from mistaken friendly fire from above also gave the NVA a ready target. Still, it couldn't be helped. Around midnight one of the jets making bomb and napalm strikes apparently touched off an enemy ammunition dump up on a ridgeline near where the NVA's 37 mm guns were located. The entire ridgeline to the south was aglow with secondary explosions as the ammo cache continued to cook off all night long.

Parnar listened to this, knowing full well that if even the smallest munitions the Americans were dropping should hit any of the CBU-100 cluster bombs lying all around him, he would be blown directly to hell. "I promised to try to be a better person if we were permitted to survive the night," he remembered later.

A bright sunrise on Tuesday, November 19, 1968 eventually burned away a heavy fog, only to reveal a heavy layer of smoke remaining from yesterday's battle. "Tom Jaeger fully expected the enemy to make a strong attack after daybreak." He had men set Claymores around their perimeter and warned the forward air controller (FAC) that Jaeger and his men should be evacuated at daybreak. The dawn brought, of all things, two North Vietnamese regulars yelling "Chu hoi!" as they moved quickly toward the American defensive position with their hands high in the air. Hatchet Force member Bog Gron found it hard to believe what he could see with his own eyes.

The Montagnards killed the one nearest the American position before the Green Berets nearby could stop them. The Americans managed to save the surviving NVA in spite of Montagnard demands that he too be killed.

Less than an hour after the Americans saved the NVA regular, the sound of incoming extraction choppers filled the air. Jaeger couldn't have been more relieved, because he'd spent the past half day multitasking, what with men who had to be rescued from a disabled chopper, first aid that had to be administered to numerous men, and not to mention the air strikes he had to call in while directing defensive operations using Claymores to encourage NVA regulars in the area to keep their distance.

As one chopper lifted off, several Americans fired their weapons into the surrounding jungle. No enemy was visible, but they apparently fired out of frustration or fear.

Collier, leading the extraction force, now encountered something that seemed unusual: His Huey helicopter landed without a shot being fired, even though he heard air strikes in the distance peppering NVA antiaircraft positions.

After detonating their last Claymores, Jaeger's exhausted men jumped on several choppers. The sense of relief Parnar felt as the Huey climbed ever higher in the air was overwhelming. Sitting on the outer edge of the chopper, he had little trouble leaning out the door toward the jungle beneath him so that the men sitting next to him couldn't see the tears trickling down his face, until the wind swept them away. And the prisoner Howard saved from the Montagnards? He helped target nine successful bombing missions in Laos.

CHAPTER 10

al-Kibar

THE SHORT, BALDING MAN CARRYING A SMALL BRIEFCASE EXPECTED TO meet with President George W. Bush in the Oval Office that morning in April 2007. Instead, he found himself talking with National Security Adviser Stephen Hadley; Hadley's assistant, Elliott Abrams; and, surprise of surprises, Dick Cheney, vice president of the United States.

Meir Dagan, then serving as the head of the Israeli spy agency known as Massad, expected to meet with Bush because that's exactly what Israeli Prime Minister Ehud Olmert had asked for just a few days before Dagan arrived in Washington. Bush no doubt was surprised by the request, because heads of state don't normally take such meetings—especially in private.

Dispensing quickly with the usual pleasantries, Dagan turned to his right, stared directly at Cheney, and announced in heavily accented English what brought him on this 5,864-mile trip to the American capital: "Syria is building a nuclear reactor. For Syria to have a nuclear weapons program, to have a nuclear weapon, is unacceptable."

That's when Dagan began the show-and-tell, by spreading several color photographs on a coffee table, according to Yaakov Katz, whose work, Shadow Strike: Inside Israel's Secret Mission to Eliminate Syrian Nuclear Power, is a primary source quoted in this chapter. "Cheney lifted one. Hadley and Abrams took another. They could clearly make out a concrete building under construction with some large pipes being installed inside. There was nothing yet that showed the building to be a nuclear reactor. It didn't have the typical dome or smokestacks, the trademarks of nuclear facilities." Realizing that the group didn't see what they were looking for, Dagan pointed out a concrete building that served as a façade, hiding what was really going on inside. The reactor was "a gas-cooled graphite-moderated reactor . . . used to produce plutonium." This structure was practically an exact replica of the Yongbyon nuclear reactor in North Korea. Dagan had dozens of other photographs, including some taken at the recent "Six Party Talks" between the United States, other Western countries, and North Korea, designed to persuade North Korea to stop its "rogue" nuclear program.

Everyone in the room was stunned, to say the least. The meeting participants knew all about how much the North Koreans coveted nuclear weapons; their first test several months ago in October 2006 was a matter of public record. But Korea assisting Syria construct its own nuclear weapon using North Korean technology? No one in the Central Intelligence Agency (CIA) or any other US government sources had anything in the files corroborating Dagan's claim.

Everyone in the room saw this as a strategic nightmare of worldwide proportions.

Israel managed to find the facility, hidden though it was, deep in the desert of northeastern Syria, along the Euphrates River. The Syrians, Dagan explained, had used the river to conceal their rogue nuclear activity. They built the reactor in a wadi, a valley, so passing cars or hikers couldn't see it. The outer square structure that surrounded the reactor was built to look like an old Ottoman-era fort, no different from the countless other old guard posts scattered through the desert.

Cheney quietly took all this in, too courteous or introverted to mention that five years ago he himself foretold this possibility. He predicted that rogue states or terrorists would find nuclear-technology sellers and either produce or resell such armaments on the black market. Cheney also predicted that the primary seller would be North Korea.

In fact, American intelligence already knew that Chon Chibu, one of the top nuclear scientists working at the Yongbyon nuclear reactor, was making frequent trips to Damascus, Syria. "In his regular intelligence briefings, Cheney periodically asked the intelligence community what Chibu was doing there and if meant that Syria and North Korea were cooperating on nuclear activity."

The American intelligence experts acknowledged that Syria and North Korea cooperated on missile technology but denied that this cooperation included nuclear collaboration, simply stating there was no evidence of it.

Years later, Cheney charitably described these events as a misinterpretation rather than an intelligence failure.

Cheney came to the vice presidency largely due to his six terms in Congress and four years as secretary of defense. Among his first assignments in early 2001 was a survey of national security challenges and threats. He was savvy enough about nuclear reactors to point out that the reactor was almost completely built and seemed, from the photos, to be just a few months away from being operational.

Cheney recalled that just after North Korea conducted its first nuclear test, Bush declared, "The transfer of nuclear weapons or material by North Korea would be considered a grave threat to the United States for which North Korea would be held fully accountable."

During a meeting the next day with General Michael Hayden, then serving as director of the CIA, Dagan handed over copies of the same photographs provided to Cheney and candidly admitted the reason for this trip. "Israel needed American assistance in understanding what role North Korea was playing in Syria. While Israel had relatively good coverage of its neighboring countries, North Korea was a big black hole for the Jewish State." Dagan also wondered why none of the Americans he'd met on this trip asked him where or how Israel snagged the photographs.

Dagan would have told the Americans that about six months earlier, lower echelon officers from the research division of the Israeli Military Intelligence Directorate, known by its Hebrew acronym Aman, came to the head of Aman, Major General Amos Yadlin, with a few bits of intelligence that, when combined, strongly suggested that Syria likely was involved in some form of nuclear development. Although Aman had the larger footprint, Mossad was responsible for conducting covert Israeli operations. And so Yadlin had asked Dagan to conduct a joint operation in order to learn more about the possible Syrian nuclear program.

Among other leads, Aman discovered the travel itinerary of one Abdul Qadeer Khan, a rogue Pakistani scientist who peddled nuclear technology across the world. Sometime prior to 2003, Israeli intelligence learned Khan helped Muammar Gaddafi initiate a nuclear program in Libya. This factoid prompted the Israelis to determine whether maybe, just maybe, Syria was starting a program of its own.

The Israelis quickly discovered a building under construction in northeast Syria not far from the Euphrates River. Aman detected the building during routine random satellite sweeps of Syria, but he could not identify its intended purpose. "The surrounding area looked like a garbage dump. There were some tents, which the Mossad would later learn were used as living quarters for the North Korean workers." What Mossad could not determine, at least initially, was whether the building under construction was a weapons factory, a arms depot, or even a nuclear reactor.

The possibility of a nuclear facility initially seemed far-fetched, because so far as was known, Syria had little if any nuclear infrastructure, beyond an atomic energy commission led by one Ibrahim Othman and operated by a small group of Syrian nuclear scientists. All the Syrians had was a tiny Chinese research reactor constructed in the 1990s. This nuclear facility, if you could even call it that, was neither large nor technologically deep enough to provide a factor for fissionable materials. Even if the Syrians had proper facilities and equipment, their present staff was operating the "mini-reactor" on average no more than two hours daily.

During early meetings on this vexing subject, Yadlin talked openly about his suspicions, while acknowledging that he had no proof at all. "Some top-secret papers were written and shared throughout the Israeli intelligence community, but they didn't amount to anything conclusive." In the meantime the Israeli intelligence community had other fish to fry, such as curbing rocket fire from the Gaza Strip, not to mention the increasing threat posed by Iran and its own nuclear program. Besides, more than a few knowledgeable Israeli intelligence operatives thought there was no reason to believe that Syria was building a nuclear reactor. Since Israel destroyed a Syrian reactor at Osirak in 1981, these Israeli intelligence operatives argued that the Syrians were more likely to construct small nuclear facilities and focus on the enrichment of uranium and refinement of plutonium. These Israelis argued that from the Syrian perspective, building an easily discoverable (and targetable) stand-alone nuclear reactor simply made no sense.

November 2006 found US Director of National Intelligence John Negroponte in Israel getting an update on Israeli intelligence assessments in advance of Olmert's trip to Washington for consultations with Bush. Negroponte started at Massad headquarters for briefings by Dagan and his staff before consulting Yadlin and his senior Aman staff. Yadlin didn't waste any time on small talk, instead turning to a satellite image of the building the Israelis discovered in the Syrian desert, expressing his deep worries that beneath the roof of this obscure building in the middle of nowhere there might be a nuclear reactor.

Negroponte remarked that Mossad officials said nothing about this potential threat earlier that very morning.

"The answer was a setback to Aman's suspicions. If the Americans didn't know about illicit nuclear activity in Syria," Yadlin reasoned, "then it was unlikely that something was actually happening there. But Yadlin refused to give up. Something wasn't right about the building. It was isolated in the middle of the desert without any real purpose. Why was the government building there?" Yadlin sensed that the Syrians had some important purpose for this building that simply remained a mystery to the Israelis. After some serious institutional bargaining, which some might characterize as bureaucratic wrangling, the Massad and Aman executives agreed upon a course of action that started with a mission to Vienna, Austria. The objective would be to break into a Vienna hotel room occupied by Khan, the nuclear technology peddler who was also a Syrian diplomat. "The young men and women sent on the mission . . . were part of the Mossad Keshet Branch, known for covert overseas operations that involved collecting data and breaking into apartments and hotel rooms." Many of them were experienced soldiers and active reservists benched during the Second Lebanon War, which recently ended, because they were considered too valuable to lose in routine combat.

This mission carried significant long-term risks. Mossad agents doing a Watergate-like break into the hotel room of a Syrian diplomat, if detected, would be a complete disaster that might well provoke an international crisis in which Israel could easily be portrayed as the wrongful aggressor. After all, not that long ago two Mossad agents were filmed in an Auckland, New Zealand courtroom answering charges that they had tried to steal a couple of passports. Before the international incident was over, Israel issued an official apology. The last thing Israel needed now was a repeat of the Auckland disaster.

Knowing this, Olmert ordered a two-team operation that very night. The first team would conduct surveillance and deal with any interference that might arise, while the second team would break into the room. Othman's laptop soon became the central focus of the entire mission. Soon, IT-savvy Israeli agents hacked the Othman laptop, replicated his files, and installed a so-called Trojan Horse giving the Israelis access to Othman's personal computer twenty-four hours a day. Soon the operation provided a significant bonus: The Israelis discovered some photographs that Othman downloaded onto his personal computer from a digital camera.

Starting the burglary took no time at all. "Within minutes, the computer was already transmitting back to Mossad headquarters in Tel Aviv. By 11:00 p.m., the operation was completed, and Israel now had a front-row seat to one of Syria's most important computers."

The Mossad sent the stolen Othman material to Aman rather than process it locally, for reasons that remain unclear. This took some time. For one thing, the Aman officer doing the review had not been informed how important it had been to get a quick assessment. In any event, after some two weeks, when the material arrived at the Mossad door in mid-March, the intelligence officers reviewing the materials were shocked and concerned.

Dagan called the Israeli prime minister's office, immediately dispensing with the usual formality of having his people call the prime minister's people. Neither Dagan's assistant nor Olmert's chief of staff were included in the process this time. He also insisted that this meeting be strictly "off the record," with Dagan speaking directly with the prime minister.

"'I need to see you urgently,' the Mossad chief told the prime minister. 'Today.'"

Olmert was already heavily scheduled for that day; this meeting was hardly convenient, because Olmert was on his way to southern Israel for discussions on the Gaza border. Still, Olmert knew that this must be important, so he suggested that Dagan meet him in Jerusalem at five o'clock. They met at Olmert's office, as scheduled, with Dagan's deputy, Tamir Pardo, in attendance. Pardo later became the head of Massad. Dagan dispensed with the formalities, sitting directly across from Olmert as he dumped and spread a large collection of photographs across the prime minister's finely polished desk.

"This is an atomic reactor and it is in Syria," Dagan announced, breathlessly, explaining that the photograph collection was acquired very recently. "In the meantime, since the operation, new satellite images had come back from Aman showing that the Syrians were in the early stages of digging a canal from the suspicious building to the Euphrates River, further proof that the building was a reactor and needed a constant flow of water to cool its core."

Stunned into silence and exasperation, Olmert asked what was to be done about this. Almost as if by coincidence, one of his publicity men burst into the room saying that within a few hours there would be an announcement of new criminal allegations against Olmert. They wanted to know what they should say? Olmert's answer was simple enough. "Tell whoever arrived with this dribble to go to hell."

Olmert paused and thought through how he, and more important, Israel, would deal with this clear and present danger. There was nothing to quibble about, much less seriously dispute, on the mahogany desk in front of him. This wasn't a report arguing one way or another about a magazine article, eye-witness account, publicly reported speech by an enemy general, or anything of that nature to which judgment had to be applied. Instead, Olmert and the others were looking at photographs establishing that the Syrian Atomic Energy Commission was constructing a nuclear reactor in Israel's backyard. Worse still, it was almost finished.

Three issues confronted Israel: Was there proof that the building in question was really a nuclear reactor? Could Israel tolerate such a thing in Syria? And if not, what could they do about it?

This was not Olmert's first dance, but this situation presented a whole new level of threat. "Syria, he understood, was building a capability that could potentially be used to try and destroy Israel. For Olmert, it was that simple. Nuclear weapons in the hands of Syria posed a direct and immediate threat the Israel could not live with. The reactor had to be eliminated." Olmert ordered Dugan to do just that—and soon.

American enthusiasm for military action in Syria was tepid at best. "No core, no war," Bush said when informed of the problem. Dagan convinced Hayden during an in-person meeting that Syria was building a nuclear reactor—called al-Kibar—but no mistakes or even exaggerations of the situation could be tolerated.

The CIA had seen all this before quite recently when, in 2003, the agency helped develop the controversial rationale supporting the invasion of Iraq and subsequent occupation. Now, in 2007, the majority of the public opposed the war. Truth be told, few government officials were any more supportive than the man on the street.

First things first—Hayden brought in CIA experts to make sure the photographs had not been enhanced or otherwise doctored before confirming the Mossad interpretation of what Israel and the United States were confronted with. Just a few years' earlier CIA satellites detected work at this very facility or one nearby. The problem was that back then the purpose of the facility could not be determined.

"The National Geospatial-Intelligence Agency, responsible for providing satellite imagery to support US intelligence operations, had classified the building as 'enigmatic,' a category within the US intelligence community that meant the target was important but had an unknown and mysterious purpose. With Dagan's photos, the purpose was now becoming clear."

One photograph that attracted more than a little attention portrayed some writing on the side of a pickup truck, which had been pixelated (rendered out of focus). Hayden covered the peculiar elements of this situation during a meeting with Bush the next day. Hayden speculated that the Israelis brought this to the attention of the CIA due to the agency's size, sophistication, assets, and capabilities. These worldwide resources often included, but not always, the ability to reach out and touch whomever might be needed in a particular project. Massad, as astute and sophisticated as it was, necessarily focused on a much smaller region and as a consequence had a greater capability to get "the details" given the greater Israeli acquaintance with the culture and even the linguistics of particular target countries.

Israel and the United States agreed that something had to be done—but deciding upon what to do took months. Eventually an Israeli attack on the assumed nuclear reactor became the proper course of action. But first, in August 2007, elite Israeli commandoes from the IDF General Staff Reconnaissance Unit, better known by its Hebrew name Sayeret Matkal, probed into Syria, getting as close to the presumed reactor as possible to obtain photographs and soil samples while proving the feasibility of a ground attack against al-Kibar.

Out in the far distance, one could see the Euphrates beyond the hills, which seemed to rise ever so slightly from the Syrian desert, or it must have seemed to the transport helicopter pilots responsible for the commandos in the cramped passenger compartments behind them. More than one transport helicopter pilot might have wondered whether it might have been better to have the attack helicopters immediately behind them go in first. There was, of course, a backup team not in the air but nearby, including a search-and-rescue team, just in case things went really, really wrong. Safest of all, the command place circled in the high altitude above them, too high to be brought down by most surface-to-air missiles, their crews listening for Syrian military communications.

The planning and implementation for this mission were shorter than usual because of what was at stake. The training began in early June 2007. Now, little more than a month later, the helicopters dropped the commandos a few dozen miles from the reactor, which was the focus of all this attention. They traveled the rest of the way in jeeps and on foot.

These commandos, called Matkalists, were ready for the mission. Just a few months before, during the 2006 "Second Lebanon War, the commandos ran a number of special operations. One brought them deep into Lebanon's Bekaa Valley, a known Hezbollah stronghold, where the [Israelis] wrongly thought two abducted reservists were being held." This time, the battle procedure was shorter, a result of the narrow window between learning about the reactor and the imposed deadline for attacking it. "The commandos boarded the helicopters knowing that as soon as they hit the ground, they would be on their own. If something went wrong, the chances of getting rescued were not particularly high."

Usually on such missions, the commandos would organize themselves into several squads, the smallest of which typically went out front and scouted what was ahead of them. The commandos stopped at the midway point of each hour to rest, but not to snack. That was done along the way, relying mostly on energy bars. No packaging was left behind, mostly as a safety precaution to prevent anyone from following their trail.

Standard procedures placed the scouts some 109 yards ahead of everyone else so that the scout commander could assess the ground ahead and motion the main body ahead with two clicks on the two-way radio being used that day.

Before the mission geologists and other scientists had briefed these men. They knew what to look for and specifically what samples to bring back for examination. When they were close enough to the reactor, the team leader gave the order and a few of the soldiers started filling plastic boxes with dirt, soil, and plants. "They had to dig deep to get the right samples. Radioactive exposure was not a concern . . ." This was so because the samples would have been relatively small.

The core mission objective was achieved in a matter of minutes. Within a few days, lab results confirmed that a nuclear reactor was definitely under construction. Briefings for Israeli, American, and British intelligence followed, as did conflicts about what to do within the Israeli government.

The dilemma seemed almost insurmountable. "If Israel attacked the reactor, it ran the risk of instigating a devastating war with Syria. If it didn't, one of its enemies would have nuclear weapons."

During the final Israeli Security Council meeting on the subject, held on September 5, 2007, the participants learned that new satellite footage confirmed that construction of the new reactor "was nearly complete, as was the digging of a water canal from the Euphrates to the reactor." Israeli intelligence believed that the facility was close to being activated. "In addition, from out of the blue, some journalists were asking questions about rumors they had heard of an impending Israeli military strike against Syria. One of the journalists worked for an American newspaper, one that was not bound by Israeli military sensor rules . . . There was no time left."

This was going to be a long meeting, disguised, as best as it could be, by a press release from the Office of the Prime Minister stating that the Security Cabinet would focus today on how to best deal with rocket attacks launched from the Gaza Strip by Hamas. The press release was routine as it parroted many more before it.

Everyone in the room knew the intelligence by heart, but Yadlin and Dagan went through it line by line anyway, using color-coded graphics to describe each phase of the operation. Red stood for high risk, yellow didn't indicate medium risk as one might think, but instead suggested low risk, according to the graph specially created for the meeting.

After that, Israeli Defense Forces Chief of Staff Gabi Ashkenazi and IAF Commander Major General Eliezer Shkedi presented the detailed operational plans, even though there was still an ongoing debate about exactly how to conduct the attack. Ashekenazi "asked the cabinet to approve the strike but to leave the decision on the way it should be carried out up to him." A trio consisting of Olmert, Defense Minister Ahud Barak, and Foreign Minister Tzipi Livni would determine the exact timing. Even as the cabinet meeting progressed, the Israeli Air Force finalized the mission preparations.

"Recognizing the significance of the moment, Olmert decided to let all of the ministers speak. It was dramatic. Each minister laid out his or her opinion, hopes and beliefs. Some expressed hesitation." Others said almost nothing. Isaac Herzog spoke for many, if not most, when he raised his hand moments later in approval, murmuring only, "May God be with us." After the meeting ended, Olmert, Barak, and Livni met in the cabinet room with several advisers to review specific attack options. Eventually Ashkenazi was the only other official left in the room to make the final recommendation. "We need to attack tonight," he whispered, as at least one of the people listening gasped. Ashkenazi continued, "A narrow airstrike would definitely destroy the reactor" and was least likely to instigate a war. After a surprisingly few minutes, Olmert, Barak, and Livni decided to do just that.

An imaginary target had been bombed in the Negev Desert for one last air force practice flight on the evening of September 4, giving the pilots going on the mission after weeks of training one last chance to hone their skills.

They gathered in a squadron training room around Shkedi, who participated in an early training mission in order to learn what this mission was really about. "Your mission is to bomb a nuclear reactor in Syria," he said, emphasizing how important this was. One can only imagine the looks on their faces.

Everyone in the room was stunned. Most, if not all of these men had flown deep behind enemy lines on top-secret missions, yet they could not imagine bombing a nuclear reactor. "Shkedi told the pilots that the operation had three objectives: destroy the reactor, return to Israel without losing any aircraft, and complete the mission as quietly as possible without detection." The mission code name, Soft Melody, was entirely appropriate.

Decades later, one pilot reflected: "It was a shock, but we didn't really have time to think about it." The men who ordered the attack monitored the operation from an underground command center called the "Bor," a nickname that in Hebrew means "pit." The War Room, the Israeli Defense Force central command center, was then configured so that the chief of staff sat in "the middle of a long table lined with computers and phones of different colors . . ." Television screens displayed feeds from naval vessels, satellites, drones, and other sources. Shkedi took his usual place in the operation communications center, right in front of a large radar screen used to track each plane, which also had separate screens showing the diminishing amounts of fuel and weapons available to each. Nearby, government officials led by the prime minister watched the operation being conducted in real time, just as they had on many previous occasions.

Eight planes assigned to the mission took off at ten thirty that evening, departing from Hatzerim Airbase in Southern Israel and the Ramon Airbase in the Negev Desert. The entire payload consisted of some twenty tons of bombs, more than enough to take out the 2,100-square-foot target building. Some of the bombs contained satellite guidance systems as an extra measure of assurance that at least some bombs would reach the target in a worst-case scenario.

Several of the pilots on the mission spent the entire time en route wondering to themselves whether somewhere in the desert surface-to-air missiles had been hidden to take them out. And of course they also worried that other things could go wrong. More than a few speculated to themselves how the next mission would be handled.

Westward they flew, far enough over the Mediterranean Sea that they just might be safe, while at the same time operating electronic warfare systems that might, just might, hide their location. A steep right turn northward toward Syria soon brought them over the border between Turkey and Syria. Much sooner than some of them had imagined, the Israelis were making their final approach to the reactor.

Now the planes began flying as low as possible, sometimes only two hundred feet over the ground in an effort to avoid Syrian detection, all the while maintaining the strictest radio silence—so strict that each pilot had to deal with any emergencies himself.

Soon enough the reactor came into sight. Just after midnight the fighters arrived at the reactor, but nobody on the ground saw them or was even looking. The pilots separated out of their formation and began to climb. Within seconds they began the deep dive toward the target.

Each plane dropped its individual load, some twenty tons in the aggregate directly over the nuclear reactor. Reverberation in the wings told each pilot in turn that the bombs he dropped had exploded, striking the roof, exterior walls, and everything within the building as cameras recorded the entire bombing phase of the operation. There was nothing surprising in what happened, the roof and sidewalls caved in, leaving the building a total wreck that could not be rebuilt or salvaged.

The whole bomb drop took two minutes or less, including the time the planes circled above watching the show. Before anyone really thought about what had just happened, the lead pilot sent word of mission accomplished back to Israel, yelling "Arizona" into his microphone.

The clapping, smiles, and hugs broke out even though the mission assessment had not yet been reported. "Shkedi could not yet relax; the pilots still had to get back home safely. By now the Syrians knew they were there, and they needed to get out quickly."

The mission had been fraught with danger, some obvious, some not so much. During their last briefing before they began, the pilots learned that they must do everything possible to avoid a direct confrontation with the Syrians. This was because Syrian President Bashar al-Assad would probably respond if one his jets went down. The Israeli Air Force could not enter the area around the nuclear reactor building—a "deniability zone"—to rescue any Israeli pilots shot down. In effect, if the operation went wrong, Israeli involvement would be completely denied.

After the strike the planes lit their boosters, streaking northward over the Syrian border with Turkey and on westward to the safety of the Mediterranean, knowing that flowing low would not provide any extra safety. Of course the Syrians launched a few missiles, but they struck nothing. The pilots were asleep in their bunks by three in the morning, some five hours after leaving to begin the strike.

Meanwhile Bashar al-Assad dozed through the whole thing in the Presidential Palace miles away in Damascus. He first heard about the destruction of his prized reactor at about one o'clock in the morning. He didn't say much to his staff.

He had to decide what, if anything, he should do about this. Was he prepared to begin a war over this single incident, however significant to his dream for a nuclear reactor and a possible nuclear weapon? Of course, the Israelis, particularly the Military Intelligence Directorate, pondered this for days if not weeks, knowing full well they could only guess what this man, however powerful, might do.

Among the possibilities considered by the Israeli Defense Force was an Assad initiative to bring in Hezbollah to strike the northern section of Israel with Katyusha rockets brought in from Lebanon. On the other hand, he might order Syrian commando units into the Golan Heights for an attack or even an occupation of an Israeli output there. The least risk, the Israeli strategists calculated, were he to do anything at all, would be firing off a missile or two aimed for no town in particular in central Israel. Anything was possible with this guy.

Back in the command center, Yadlin and perhaps others, guessed that "Assad would let this [the reactor attack] slide just as he had done after other Israeli incursions over the years."

And in the end, that is exactly what he did.

CHAPTER 11

The White Horse

Between 600,000 and 750,000 Palestinians fled or were driven out of the territory upon which the State of Israel was established and which it conquered during the war of 1948–1949. The Arabs vowed to destroy the newborn state and the Israeli leadership believed that if their precarious, vulnerable country was to have any chance of surviving, there had to be as few Arabs as possible within its borders. This was the rationale, however morally questionable, behind both the expulsions and the blanket refusal to allow any refugees to return—ever.

—RONEN BERGMAN, *RISE AND KILL FIRST*

As the years went by the dominant regimes bordering Israel claimed that the Zionists would ultimately be treated as the Palestinians had been, removed so that the Palestinians could once again live on land that had been theirs. All the while these braggarts "imposed harsh conditions on the unfortunate refugees, who often had no rights, no significant control of their own lives, no prospects for higher education or worthy employment." So says Ronen Bergman, whose work *Rise and Kill First*, served as a primary source quoted in this chapter.

The population of the Gaza Strip, some 140 square miles in what the British had designated Mandatory Palestine some twenty-eight years earlier, tripled overnight, or so it seemed. Others settled in makeshift camps in the West Bank, land occupied by Jordan after the 1948 Arab-Israeli War and re-occupied by Israel in 1967. More still established slap-dash camps in Arab countries near Israel.

Now stateless, having lost their own country and being welcomed by no other, the Palestinian refugees encamped in West Bank and Gaza camps, towns, cities, and villages persevered, considering themselves to be a people. And in the worst camps the youngest among them, conflicted by pride and hatred, organized into nationalist movements.

Khalil al-Wazir led his own militant group in a Gaza refugee camp by the time he was sixteen. Deported from Ramla, some fifteen miles southeast of Tel Aviv, in 1948, Palestinian veterans of the war that year trained al-Wazir and his two-hundred-man unit in sabotage and terror. Mohammed Yasser Abdel Rahman Raouf Arafat al Qudwa al-Husseini, soon known simply as Yasser Arafat, joined the reinforcements soon sent to al-Wazir for training and deployment.

And there lies a small mystery. Official Palestinian history records that Arafat was born in Jerusalem in 1929—no surprise there. Arafat came from a significant Palestinian family whose distant and not-so-distant relatives included Abd al-Qadir al-Husseini, the very man who in 1948 commanded Palestinian forces. He was also related to the Grand Mufti, Hajj Amin al-Husseini. In the years since, alternative history has placed Arafat's place of birth as Gaza or even Cairo. Taking anonymous noms de guerre, al-Wazir, now called Abu Jihad, and Yasser Arafat, now known as Abu Ammar, soon began working as a team, strengthening Palestinian guerrilla operations throughout the Strip.

Years later, one Israeli intelligence officer remembered the Palestinian forces in those early years as insignificant and ineffective. This Israeli considered Palestinians militarily significant only to when they quietly crossed into the new state of Israel to kill and otherwise harass the Jewish inhabitants. Eight years after the United Nations established Israel, the Egyptian government refused to continue sponsoring Palestinian military missions into Israel. Palestinian fortunes declined ever more when the Israelis achieved victory in the Sinai Campaign, the only silver lining from a Palestinian perspective being the creation of a Palestinian guerrilla movement.

Finally, Arafat and Abu Jihad relocated to Kuwait in late 1959 after tiresome, frustrating years roaming from country to country seeking help. Gradually they began to see that Nasser, himself focused on unification among Arabs, saw Arafat and Abu Jihad not as allies but barriers. This convinced them to stop seeking help in major Arab states that had no interest in an exclusively Palestinian organization under their leadership.

Even though he personally recruited and trained him, Abu Jihad recruited Arafat, some six years or so older than himself, to become a Palestinian leader, due largely to his extensive network of connections across the Palestinian diaspora. Arafat in turn could see that Abu Jihad was better equipped than himself to organize, lead, and conduct operations. Once they had settled on their own division of responsibilities, Abu Jihad and Arafat worked with a yet unidentified group of fellow believers drafting and refining goals, objectives, strategies, and tactics for a Palestinian state, working in secret in order to avoid the wrath of the Arab states around them. They established the Palestinian Liberation Movement (PLM) in mid-October 1959.

The PLM was eventually renamed Fatah ("Victory"). Soon thereafter they discovered that the Arabic acronym of Fatah is "quick death," hardly a recruiting tool in the Arabic community. Once this was discovered, Abu Jihad quickly changed the Arabic acronym to Fatah, meaning "glorious victory."

Preoccupied with Egypt, Israeli intelligence missed the Fatah founding. "It wasn't until early 1964, more than four years after the fact, that two Israeli spies" filed reports suggesting that "cells of students functioning with Fatah's support and inspiration were gaining more and more momentum in Europe . . ." In early April, an Israeli intelligence analyst expressed the opinion that educated Palestinian scholars and students presented just as much of a threat as neighboring Arab states, even those possessing or with access to weapons of mass destruction. Israelis assigned to study Abu Jihad and Arafat had no trouble concluding that both men were capable of inspiring large-scale Palestinian military and quasi-military action against Israel.

That same year, Abu Jihad journeyed to China and East Asia. His Fatah pitch supposedly enchanted Zhou Enlai, other communists in North Korea and Vietnam, and even Che Guevara whom Abu Jihad met in Algiers.

The first day of 1965 brought the maiden Fatah attack on a massive water system designed to dampen dry southern Israel with water from the Sea of Galilee.

There was no mistaking Abu Jihad's objective, although contemporaries viewed his strategy and tactics as designed for nothing less than utter failure. Abu Jihad hoped to cut off a certain Israeli water supply in the desert, but his efforts were amateur and, in the view of many, practically designed for failure. Worse yet, at least from a Palestinian perspective, the whole operation had to be canceled when authorities arrested Fatah members several days before the operation launch date.

Authorities in Lebanon apprehended a second element of the strike force a few days later, leaving several Fatah members from Jordan to act alone, only to watch the explosives fail to detonate just before they were arrested by a security patrol. Abu Jihad settled in Damascus that year.

Despite this calamity Palestinian students then living in Germany and elsewhere in Europe swelled the Fatah ranks, even as Mossad began electronic monitoring across Europe. Ineffective as Fatah was in those early months, some Mossad elements advocated assassinating the entire leadership cadre, including Abu Jihad, but were turned down on the theory that Fatah was little more than a street gang. Early January 1966 brought forty Fatah attacks upon Israel itself—changing that perception of Fatah as a marginal organization forever.

The defeat of Arab states in the early June 1967 Six Day War brought a loss of Arab prestige in the Palestinian community, strengthening the Palestinian Liberation Organization (PLO). Fatah joined the PLO that very year and soon became the predominant PLO faction, thus strengthening the personal power of Abu Jihad. Shortly thereafter he organized, trained, and recruited al-Assifa, which became the armed wing of Fatah, bringing him additional duties conducting guerrilla operations in the occupied Palestinian lands and Israel itself.

Eight years, and many operations later, Abu Jihad, according to many but not all sources, planned and coordinated an attack on the Savoy Hotel in Tel Aviv on the evening of March 4 in which eight Israeli hostages and three Israeli soldiers lost their lives. Three years later, Abu Jihad planned the March 1978 Coastal Road Massacre in which thirty-five civilians aboard a bus were murdered.

After planning an unsuccessful response to the mid-1982 Israeli siege of Beirut, Lebanon, Abu Jihad relocated to Jordan while most of the PLO leadership fled to Tunis. He began establishing youth organizations, which, under his guidance in 1987, initiated a five-year Palestinian uprising against the Israeli occupation of the West Bank and Gaza called the Intifada, or "shaking off" in Arabic.

On March 14, 1988, the Israeli security cabinet met once again on an old subject. Through the years at least three Israeli prime ministers approved plans to kill Abu Jihad, but that had not happened. Prime Minister Yitzhak

Shamir considered his options and the political risks that confronted him in making such a decision.

Strategically speaking, Shamir faced a major challenge, because Abu Jihad was by no means an ordinary target with minimum risk of retaliation. Shamir had to explain and justify this proposal to an approval committee consisting of ten ministers, five from Likud and five from Labor. The head of the Labor Party, Shimon Perez, opposed the kill on very practical grounds, because intelligence reports in his possession suggested that Abu Jihad, despite his name, was a moderate who might, from time to time, temper the more vigorous and violence-prone Palestinian factions. Perez was not the only opponent. Several others worried about subsequent international reaction and possible sanctions should the operation go forward. Initially there appeared to be a tied vote, meaning the operation would not go forward.

No one could have guessed what happened next. "Look at what Intifada is doing to us," Moshe Nissim, the Likud finance minister, said to Defense Minister Yitzhak Rabin after asking him to have a private conversation in the meeting room while others continued the group discussions. Nissim described the Israeli public mood as "despondent." He worried about public perception, in Israel and the rest of the world, about the effectiveness of the Israeli Defense Force (IDF), saying that from Nissim's perspective, the IDF hadn't had a real victory in a long time. Nissim saw a need for the IDF to carry out a noteworthy, successful mission in order to restore national Israeli morale. Better yet, the killing of Abu Jihad, from the perspective of Nissim, would be a proper blood sacrifice whose objective was more symbolic than moral.

Seconds later both men returned to the meeting room. Nissim told everyone present that he was changing his vote. The larger group approved inaptly named Operation Introductory Lesson by a vote of six to four. Nissim, who was the son of the Chief Rabbi of Israel, would never regret that he'd persuaded Rabin. "In the whole world," he said, "there isn't another army that is as meticulous as the IDF about values and norms of conduct and assuring that innocent people aren't hurt." Yet there is a Talmudic precept: If a man comes to kill you, rise early and kill him first.

You couldn't ask for a better place to kill Abu Jihad than his hometown in Tunisia

The home of the revolutionary Abu Jihad was on the corner in a tony neighborhood of broad, sparkling clean streets about a mile from the beach, providing the assassins multiple escape options, once they could overcome the team of two (yes, only two) guards protecting Abu Jihad. The advantages of this venue were immediately obvious: "a relatively isolated location only lightly guarded." That description by a highly ranked Israeli intelligence officer said it all. Better yet, the Israelis confirmed that when Abu Jihad was in Tunisia he invariably slept at home. This venue could not have been better suited for the kill.

Apparently, the target felt very safe in Tunisia, since, as far as was known, the Israelis had never conducted an operation there. Beyond this was an important strategic consideration. "Killing Abu Jihad in his home would also be suitably menacing, suggesting to the Palestinians that no one was safe anywhere." Perhaps best of all, a plan had already been developed the previous year.

Two Israeli (Aman) military intelligence units working with Massad began tracking Abu Jihad on a daily basis. They spotted one peculiarity almost immediately: Abu Jihad purchased tickets on multiple flights to multiple destinations every time he traveled. This added to the difficulty of knowing where he was at any given time. Naturally, the Israelis tapped his home and office telephones, but then again, Abu Jihad all but certainly would have assumed this and acted accordingly. Israeli intelligence mapped his neighborhood in great detail, while three "Arab businessmen" (Israeli operatives) identified all routes leading to the Jihad residence. While conducting these and other operations against Abu Jihad, Oded Raz, an Aman officer specializing in terrorism, couldn't help but notice that setting aside his hatred of Israel, in all respects Abu Jihad possessed admirable qualities, both as an authentically gifted military leader and family man.

That said, he was behind the death of hundreds of Jews and a direct threat to Israel. Rabin expressed doubts about the operation, concerned as he was with the safety of the assassins. He also wondered what would happen if Abu Jihad wasn't home. After the Mossad operators explained in detail their method of avoiding just such a disaster, Rabin approved Operation Introductory Lesson.

Barak asked about the possibility of a "two-for-one" operation in which one of Abu Jihad's neighbors, another PLO terrorist code-named Abu Mazen, would also be killed. In the end Mossad convinced Barak that however easy the second kill might seem in the operations room, as a practical matter, killing Mazen would overcomplicate an already difficult mission.

The first six operatives arrived in Tunis, then a city of 2.7 million souls on Thursday, April 14, 1988, on four different planes. Three of them—two men and one woman—carried false passports from Lebanon. Speaking the perfect French that many Beirutians boasted in that era, they paid cash to rent two Volkswagen vans and a Peugeot 305 sedan. The vehicles, all white in color, had been rented from different companies. The plan called for the Sayeret Matkal operators to be driven from the beach to the Jihad residence and returned to the place they started. Three additional operatives working as "shadows" would observe undetected from a clump of trees nearby to make sure that Abu Jihad was inside his home. Once the mission was accomplished, the main team would return to the beach, while the shadows would leave Tunis later on commercial flights.

Even then, a mobile hospital, communications equipment, and other supplies aboard five Israeli missile boats steamed toward Tunisia alongside a larger vessel disguised as a cargo ship—the "cargo" being a helicopter. The convoy pulled up twenty-five miles from the coast, well beyond the territorial waters of Tunisia on April 15. "Below, in the water, the Israeli submarine Gal provided a quiet, invisible escort. Far above, an air force Boeing 707 served as a communications relay station, while also monitoring Tunisian frequencies for any trouble."

Equipment on that same plane could also jam Tunisian air control or radar if that became necessary. Israeli F-15s flew just above the coastal waters, just in case. All seemed quiet enough when several rubber dinghies holding two commandos and six Sayeret Matkal soldiers launched and moved toward the sun, sinking into the western horizon. While they moved out, seven more commandoes from Flotilla 13 quietly slipped into the water from their dinghies and moved underwater toward the beach from a third of a mile away. Yoav Galant, the Flotilla 13 raiding force, was the first to set foot on Tunisian soil. They stretched their line out in a semicircle, waiting in this defensive perimeter as the radio operators contacted the Mossad drivers who would take them to the target.

Now on the beach, the soldiers ran toward the waiting cars, where they traded damp duds for the dry clothes they had carried in waterproof duffel bags. Now the crew, mostly male but with a few females among them, headed toward the Jihad residence where they would quietly (they hoped) break down a door and kill Abu Jihad. Aware that at least some of them might be captured, they all carried POW cards to prove that they were military personnel, "just in case," knowing full well that this paperwork might not make much difference in how they were treated.

Just about then the naval commandos spread themselves all along the beach perimeter while waiting for the hit squad to return. Three Caesarea covert operators, who earlier conducted surveillance, now trained their high-quality binoculars on a vehicle carrying Abu Jihad as it quietly pulled into the driveway just after midnight. As they expected, the driver escorted another bodyguard and Abu Jihad into the house, before returning to the car to sleep. The other bodyguard stayed briefly in the living room before walking down to the basement for the night. Soon, as predicted, both bodyguards were dozing away.

Unaware of his fate, Abu Jihad went to his bedroom, told his wife he wasn't tired, and began writing a letter to the Intifada leadership as their sixteen-year-old daughter Inan watched. Later, another daughter named Hanan recalled a dream she had had the previous night. In the dream, she had been praying at a mosque with a few friends when suddenly Israeli soldiers burst into the mosque and began chasing her and her friends. While running outside the city walls, she lost the soldiers and then noticed her father passing by. She stopped, said hello, and asked him where he was going. He told her he was on his way to Jerusalem. She asked how he could get past all the Israeli soldiers walking around just outside the town walls. He told her that he would ride past them on a white horse. So went the dream.

Then came a complication for the Israelis, who planned to kill Abu Jihad at one thirty. Having tapped the villa phone, the Israelis were alarmed to hear one of Abu Jihad's aides tell him that a seat on a three o'clock flight from Tunis to Baghdad had been booked for him. Knowing that Abu Jihad would have to leave for the airport by one o'clock in the morning in order to get through security, they realized that their plan to kill him at one thirty was out the window.

The Israelis had to act now. Speaking in code, the operators on the ground outside the Abu Jihad villa received permission to do just that. With that, the two vans carried some twenty-six Israelis carrying Micro Uzi and Ruger .22 pistols into the area for the kill. All the weapons were equipped with silencers. A couple consisting of a man and a woman disguised as locals carefully drove the Peugeot under the local speed limit to assess the situation ahead and assure the rest of the crew that there wouldn't be any surprises.

They stopped some five hundred yards from the villa; within seconds the commandos silently moved toward the target, even as those supervising the mission fretted about getting final, positive identification. Nothing, absolutely nothing, had been left to chance. Just as they'd seen earlier, two operatives watched Abu Jihad and his men go into the house. That said, Rabin had agreed to a protocol that, as a practical matter, required that someone with expertise in Arabic listen for hours to tapes of Abu Jihad speaking, to confirm beyond any doubt that this in fact was the man to be killed. In order to achieve this, the designated listeners wearing earphones as they relaxed in the Tel Aviv command bunker, themselves fluent Arabic speakers from Unit 8200, spent hour upon hour studying Abu Jihad's voice. They intercepted a telephone connection from Italy that Abu Jihad frequently used to communicate with his subordinates across the occupied territories. After confirming his identity, one of the Israeli operatives called Abu Jihad, claiming in an erratic, distressed voice that one of Abu Jihad's key operators, Abu Rahma, was going to prison with his entire family. Even as Abu Jihad tried to calm the caller and get more information about the fake arrest, Israeli experts were verifying his voice patterns so the kill could be completed.

Before anyone expected, Tel Aviv green-lighted the mission. Seconds later, two Israeli soldiers dressed as women approached the first guard, then sitting by himself in a car parked next to the house. One of the disguised soldiers took out a hotel brochure, showed it to the guard, and asked how to get there. Not knowing any better, the guard studied the map as Lev quietly and quickly pulled a pistol equipped with a silencer out of a large candy box and shot him once in the head.

Now came the loud part. Lev motioned the door-opening team forward with the hydraulic jack that opened the front door slightly with a loud creak, even as backup teams surrounded the house and positioned themselves in the back yard. And then the tough part began.

The Israeli operators had no time to waste. Breaking down the door, they raced down the hall as a few of them broke off and rushed into the basement, just in time to kill the second bodyguard before he was fully awake and able to cock his rifle. They also spotted the family gardener, who had decided to spend the night. Within seconds, he was dead. "He really hadn't done anything, but on a mission like this there's no choice. You have to make sure that any potential opposition is neutralized," Lev said after the mission was completed.

Masked Sayeret Matkal operators clad in black were bounding up the stairs toward the target. Abu Jihad pushed his wife as far back in the bedroom away from the bedroom door as was possible, just as the first Israeli shot him. The force of the bullet knocked Abu Jihad to the floor. Lev now killed him with a long burst, but five Israeli commandos shot him too, just to make sure. Later, someone determined that he had been shot fifty-two times in all.

And with that the Israeli commandos escaped, that task made easier by a series of bogus calls claiming that dozens of Israeli operatives were racing toward the very center of Tunis. The police set up dozens of roadblocks and searched every vehicle moving, only to discover the rented Volkswagens and Peugeot abandoned far away from downtown Tunis on a beach.

The next day, Shamir told a reporter asking about the targeted assassination that he'd heard about it on the radio. Within a week the Palestinians, led by Arafat, buried Abu Jihad with full military honors.

While the Abu Jihad assassination seemed a good idea at the time and briefly impaired PLO military capability, Israeli intelligence later considered it a failure for one reason. Killing Abu Jihad did not dampen the Intifada as hoped, but instead fanned the Intifada flames. Ronen believed "the elimination of Abu Jihad greatly weakened the PLO leadership but bolstered the Popular Committees in the occupied territories which were the true leaders of the uprising."

Bergman noted in 2018 that many Israeli participants in the Abu Jihad assassination now regretted it for a reason that seems surprising to many. A number of savvy Israeli operators continued to believe that Abu Jihad was a force for good, in the sense that although he was an enemy, he was an enemy who often acted affirmatively to restrain and limit the violent tendencies that Arafat all too often acted upon. Decades later many of these dissenters speculated that after the 1974 establishment of the Palestinian National Authority, Abu Jihad might well have restrained Hamas and prevented it from becoming the dominant Palestinian force which threatened Israel.

Yet another prominent Israeli, Amnon Lipkin-Shahak, who later became chief of the Israeli General Staff, remarked, "If we had known that a short time after Abu Jihad's elimination, the PLO would take the diplomatic course, then perhaps we would have raided his house and first of all talked with him about his attitudes toward a compromise with Israel and then decided whether to kill him or not. In retrospect, his absence is indeed evident to a certain extent. He could have made a significant contribution to the peace process."

That said, recalling the assassination many years later, in 2013, Moshe Ya'alon, at that time minister of Israeli defense, called the operation the perfect hit. "I don't understand why they say we, Israel are (sic) losing the war for minds. If I put a bullet between Abu Jihad's eyes, right in the middle of his mind, doesn't that mean that I've won?"

Reader's choice.

CHAPTER 12

Death Comes for al-Baghdadi

THERE WAS NO MISTAKING THE NOISES ABOVE THEM, WHICH TURNED after-dinner banter into terror. Their host was a middle-aged man in an almost-new compound at a Barisha, a border town of some seven thousand souls in western Syria, about three miles from the border with Turkey. Now, an hour before midnight, local time on Saturday, October 26, 2019, the whirring sound of chopper blades made them all run for their lives.

About a half hour earlier, upon arriving back at the White House at four thirty in the afternoon after playing golf in the Virginia countryside, President Donald J. Trump learned the good news. A positive ID had been made on an ISIS leader the United States had wanted to find for at least half a decade. This was hardly a surprise, because the military told Trump they had a strong lead on Abu Bakr al-Baghdadi's whereabouts some three days earlier, as recounted in the November 2, 2019 *London Times* article, "Jackpot: the inside story of how US tracked and killed Baghdadi," by Catherine Philp, "Jackpot" serves as a primary source for this chapter, except where otherwise indicated.

Trump walked quickly to the White House Situation Room, where Vice President Mike Pence, Defense Secretary Mark Esper, National Security Adviser Robert O'Brien, and a host of intelligence officials joined them for the show.

At least that's the way Trump described it, claiming later that as he watched the operation unfold on satellite television, it seemed as if they were watching a movie. The target was ISIS leader Abu Bakr al-Baghdadi. And whether this multi-million-dollar military operation focused on a single man was fate or fortune, it all began in the summer of 1971 in Samarra, Iraq, at the time a city of some 119,000 souls on the banks of the Tigris River.

Although no one knows for sure, most investigators believe that the man called Abu Bakr al-Baghdadi through most of his career was born in or near Samarra in late July 1971, the son and grandson of farmers with a strong interest in Islam. His grandfather reportedly died at age ninety-four. A Baghdadi uncle served in the Saddam Hussein security services. Years later, two Baghdadi brothers served in the Hussein army. One died in either the Iran-Iraq War or the Gulf War.

Initially interested in religious studies more than warfare, Baghdadi was no natural scholar. Investigators reviewing his educational records learned that he graduated from high school only after taking his final examination twice. In fairness, he scored 80 percent on his second try.

Unqualified for Iraqi military service due to near-sightedness and deemed unqualified for the study of law, science, or language by the University of Baghdad due to low high school grades, Baghdadi turned to Islamic studies. Some sources claim that he received three degrees in that subject.

Contemporaries interviewed for a December 27, 2014 article in the *Daily Telegraph* portrayed Baghdadi as a quiet, religious youth who spent his early years living in a small suburban Baghdad mosque. One acquaintance, himself a self-proclaimed intimate of eventual al-Qaeda leader Al-Zahrawi, described Baghdadi as "insignificant" in 2003. That said, there is little dispute that after the mid-March 2003 American invasion of Iraq he co-founded a militant group in which he served as head of the Sharia law committee.

Brought to the attention of American occupation authorities, he was arrested in early February 2004 and detained at the Camp Bucca detention center in a medium-security Sunni compound with future ISIS leaders.

In 2006 Baghdadi was serving as supervisor of the Sharia law committee in a group soon renamed ISIS. Four years later, in May 2010, he became leader of the Islamic State of Iraq (ISIL) and began masterminding large-scale terrorist operations, notably including a late-August 2011 suicide bombing at the Umm al-Qura Mosque in Baghdad in which a leading Sunni lawmaker was killed. After another twenty-three similar attacks he ordered south of Baghdad, a bounty for his capture was announced. That didn't stop him in 2011 from spearheading attacks south of Baghdad, in Mosul, and eventually in Baghdad itself, which claimed at least ninety-five lives.

Following his 2013 expansion of terrorist operations into Syria, the 2014 establishment of a worldwide caliphate with Baghdadi designated as its caliph, creation of yet another new organization called the Islamic State, and his mid-August 2015 announcement of a "marriage" with American hostage Kayla Mueller, who was subsequently murdered by ISIL, the United States increased its efforts to kill or capture him.

The Pentagon spent years searching for Baghdadi in all the wrong places based on the totally logical belief that he likely was hiding on the Iraq-Syria border near Samarra, where he was born. That pursuit began in earnest after the March 2019 occupation of Baghouz, Syria, the last ISIS stronghold.

Before that, Americans relied on ISIS prisoners, notably one Umm Sayyaf, who was captured in 2015 for information about Baghdadi whereabouts. She was the widow of a prominent Baghdadi intimate complicit in the death by rape of American Kayla Mueller, for whom the Baghdadi search mission was ultimately named.

Sayyaf knew enough about Baghdadi's general habits, methods, and preferences to kick off the search, but the first real lead was a handful of receipts (yes, receipts) picked up in ISIS structures located in eastern Syria proving payments to Hurras al-Din, an al Qaeda–affiliate organization that prepared safe houses for ISIS fighters.

Knowing full well that the Americans were on his trail, Baghdadi gradually narrowed his ever-smaller circle of ISIS contacts until only a handful were left. Perhaps of necessity, these included official ISIS spokesperson Abu Hassan al-Muhajir and a senior ISIS security official we'll simply call the "Embedded Informant."

General Mazloum Abdi, a senior official in the Kurdish-led Syrian Democratic Forces (SDF) financed by the United States, told one media source that the Embedded Informant no longer believed in ISIS and sought revenge against the organization itself and Baghdadi personally. This was so because some of the Embedded Informant's relatives had been abused by ISIS for no reason. The Embedded Informant contacted the SDF in early 2019. April brought the news that Baghdadi was in the Idlib Governate, a province west of Aleppo, Syria, controlled by ISIS nemesis and arch-rival Hayat Tahrir al-Sham. The Embedded Informant, one of the few men Baghdadi still trusted, visited Baghdadi there several times. Due to his high ISIS rank, he was not required to wear a blindfold on these trips to Idlib and used this opportunity to get a general sense of where he was being taken.

In July 2019 Baghdadi came to his last compound just outside Barisha, built the previous year by Abu Mohammed al-Halabit, a senior official of Hurras al-Din, an organization that rivaled ISIS, even though some individuals were also loosely affiliated with ISIS. A neighbor named Abu Mustafa brought his family here some three months earlier, looking for a quiet, safe place for his family to live. Mustafa and his immediate family moved into his brother's house some 328 yards from the Halabit complex.

After several visits, the Embedded Informant guessed or learned that Baghdadi's new digs were at a compound built in 2018 by Halabi. Eventually the Embedded Informant memorized the compound layout and escape routes, discovering along the way that an underground tunnel served as a hiding place but was not a means of escape. The Embedded Informant even managed to get a pair of Baghdadi's underpants, enabling the Americans to match his DNA with samples obtained fifteen years earlier when Baghdadi was a guest of the United States in Camp Bucca.

This was enough proof to initiate preparations for the mission, which began with construction of a Barisha compound replica outside the US airbase near Arbil, Iraq in a Kurdish region. The *London Times* later reported that at just about this time, the Embedded Informant also delivered some bad news. "Soon" Baghdadi would be moving to a new safe house in Jarabulus, some 105 miles to the northeast.

About four days before the raid, American military leaders went to the White House for "the ask." Trump authorized a Saturday night raid designated "Operation Kayla Mueller," laying the foundation for eight Black Hawk and Chinook helicopters protected by Apache helicopters to leave Iraq for a Syrian attack staging area. Fighter aircraft from Kuwait, six armed drones, and five guided missile cruisers and destroyers also supported the mission on a standby basis.

Some 6,035 miles away in Arbil, Kurdish Northern Iraq and al-Asad Airbase nearby, Americans prepared for the mission. About thirty of the military personnel involved were from Delta Force, while another sixty or so were Army Rangers, supported by unidentified military aircraft, ships, dogs, and even a military robot. They were all trained to maximize the chances of capturing rather than killing high-value targets, like the caliph of ISIS.

Both Turkish and Russian military forces in the area had been tipped off and agreed to hold their fire during the American flyover on the way to the target. Some seventy minutes after starting the mission, the American forces looked down on the Barisha compound, even as several locals, apparently believing that Syrian government forces had arrived, aimed their weapons upward. These ISIS fighters were no match for the Americans on the choppers who killed them all.

Seconds later, some sixty Rangers fanned out around the compound so that Delta Force specialists could blast a hole through the exterior wall. A local translator yelled that any noncombatants should come out and surrender, prompting two men and some eleven children to run outside, just as five ISIS fighters, four of whom were women, charged the Americans.

The fighters found death instead of victory as Conan the Delta Force combat dog began looking for Baghdadi.

Baghdadi, now in his mid-forties, bore an uncanny resemble to Saddam Hussein, the former president of Iraq hanged a decade ago in July 2009. This somehow seems appropriate, because most experts agree that Baghdadi, in hiding though he was in late 2019, served as the recognized caliph of the Islamic State, which Americans and most other Westerners know as ISIS. The caliph was considered the successor of Muhammed, in a tradition that dates back to the prophet himself, who Baghdadi claimed as one of his biological ancestors.

This honorific did Baghdadi little good as he fitted himself into a snug vest loaded with explosives, grabbed three of his own children, and ran for a tunnel under the complex. No doubt he hoped that he might, just might, have a chance to hide from the Americans long enough to survive all this, not knowing what the Americans had planned for him.

Confronted with a fearless fifty-five-pound Belgian Malinois canine, Baghdadi pulled the cord on his suicide vest, killing two of his own children before either reached the age of twelve, as well as blowing his own head off on his way to paradise. A quick visual inspection minutes later confirmed the Baghdadi identity.

Moments later the ISIS member who betrayed him savored watching Delta Force members load Baghdadi body parts onto a chopper. Two hours after landing at the Barisha compound, the choppers, loaded down with Baghdadi body parts, laptops, cell phones, and three prisoners thought to be the compound owner, his son, and the Embedded Informant lifted into the sky, lingering only long enough to flatten the compound.

Eventually Americans aboard USS *Lewis B. Puller* buried Baghdadi at sea in full compliance with Islamic ritual after verifying his identity through DNA tests.

The Americans made it all look easy, but this mission was anything but, given the background and terrorist career of the man the American forces had come to kill.

The long-term consequences of the Baghdadi mission have been the subject of much discussion. In "5 lessons from the death of Baghdadi," an October 29, 2019 Brookings Institution article, the editor summarized an analysis by Daniel L. Byman. The author readily admitted the most details about the raid remained elusive, for the obvious reason that the Israelis might want to use those specific tactics again. He summarized the overall impact of killing Baghdadi as illustrating that when the United States (and by implication, Israel) wishes to fight al-Qaeda and the Islamic State and places that objective at the top of its priority list, good things happen.

Conan the warrior dog was injured by electrical wires in the tunnel beneath the Barisha compound as a consequence of Baghdadi activating his explosive vest. He survived to be honored at the White House.

BIBLIOGRAPHY

Books

Alexander, Larry. *Shadows in the Jungle: The Alamo Scouts Behind Japanese Lines in World War II.* New York: New American Library, 2009.

Bascomb, Neal. *The Winter Fortress: The Epic Mission to Sabotage Hitler's Atomic Bomb.* Boston: Houghton Mifflin Harcourt, 2016

Bergman, Ronen. *Rise and Kill First: The Secret History of Israel's Targeted Assassinations.* New York: Random House, 2018.

Bohning, Don. *The Castro Obsession: US Covert Operations against Cuba, 1959–1965.* Washington, DC: Potomac Books, Inc., 2005.

Carney, Col., John T. *No Room for Error: The Covert Operations of America's Special Tactics Units from Iran to Afghanistan.* New York: Presidio Press, 2002.

Clark, William Bell. *Ben Franklin's Privateers: A Naval Epic of the American Revolution.* Baton Rouge, LA: Louisiana State University Press, 1956.

Cusick, James G. *The Other War of 1812: The Patriot War and the Invasion of Spanish East Florida.* Athens, GA: University of Georgia Press, 2003.

Dean, Josh. *The Taking of K-129: How the C.I.A. Used Howard Hughes to Steal a Russian Sub in the Most Daring Covert Operation in History.* New York: Dutton, 2017.

Geraghty, Tony. *Black Ops: The Rise of Special Forces in the C.I.A., the S.A.S. and Massad.* New York: Pegasus Books, 2010.

Gerwarth, Robert. *Hitler's Hangman: The Life of Heydrich.* New Haven and London: Yale University Press, 2011.

Gillespie, Robert M. *Black Ops Vietnam: The Operational History of MACVSOG.* Annapolis, MD: Naval Institute Press, 2011.

Harclerode, Peter. *Fighting Dirty: The Inside Story of Covert Operations from Ho Chi Minh to Osama Bin Laden.* London: Cassell Military Paperbacks, 2001.

Hogan, David W. Jr. *US Army Special Operations in World War II.* Washington, DC, Center of Military History, Department of the Army, 1992.

James, Jessica. *The Gray Ghost of Civil War Virginia: John Singleton Mosby.* Gettysburg, PA: Patriot Press, 2013.

Kagan, Neal. *The Secret History of World War II: Spies, Code Breakers and Covert Operations.* Washington, DC: National Geographic, 2016.

Katz, Yaakov. *Shadow Strike: Inside Israel's Secret Mission to Eliminate Syrian Nuclear Power.* New York: St. Martin's Press, 2019.

MacDonald, Calum. *The Assassination of Reinhard Heydrich.* Edinburgh, Scotland: Birlinn, Limited, 2007.

Maurik, E.H. Van. *From Operation Anthropoid to France: The Memoirs of E.H. Van Maurik.* Barnsley, S. Yorkshire, England: Pen & Sword Books, Ltd., 2018.

McRaven, William H. *Sea Stories: My Life in Special Operations.* New York: Grand Central Publishing, 2019.

McRaven, William H. *Spec Ops: Case Studies in Special Operations Warfare, Theory and Practice.* Novato, CA: Presidio Press, 1995.

Moore, Steven L. *Uncommon Valor: The Recon Company That Earned Five Medals of Honor and Included America's Most Decorated Green Beret.* Annapolis, MD: Naval Institute Press, September 1, 2018.

Mosby, John S. *The Memoirs of Col. John S. Mosby.* New York: Bantam Domain, 1992.

O'Toole, G. J. *An Honorable Treachery: A History of US Intelligence Espionage and Covert Action from the American Revolution to the C.I.A.* New York: Grove Press, 1991.

Pavlovsky, Arnold M. *In Pursuit of a Phantom: John Singleton Mosby's Civil War.* Amazon Digital Services, 2008.

Plaster, John L. *SOG: The Secret Wars of America's Commandos in Vietnam.* New York: Simon & Schuster, 1997.

Pushies, Fred. *US Special Ops: The History, Weapons and Missions of Elite Military Forces.* Minneapolis, MN: Quarto Publishing Group, 2016.

Rositzke, Harry. *The C.I.A.'s Secret Operations.* New York: Reader's Digest Press, 1977.

Scahill, Jeremy. *Dirty Wars: The World Is a Battlefield.* New York: Nation Books, 2013.

Schiff, Stacy. *A Great Improvisation: Franklin, France and the Birth of America.* New York: Henry Holt and Company, 2005.

Scott, John S. *Partisan Life with Mosby's Rangers.* Independently published, 2016.

Siepel, Kevin H. *Rebel: The Life and Times of John Singleton Mosby.* New York: St. Martin's Press, 1983.

Thomas, Evan. *John Paul Jones: Sailor, Hero, Father of the American Navy.* New York: Simon & Schuster, 2003.

Trimble, Lee. *Beyond the Call: The True Story of One World War II Pilot's Covert Mission to Rescue POWs on the Eastern Front.* New York: Berkley Caliber, 2015.

Williams, Joseph A. *The Sunken Gold: A Story of World War I Espionage and the Greatest Treasure Salvage in History.* Chicago: Chicago Review Press Incorporated, 2017.

Zedric, Lance Q. *Silent No More: The Alamo Scouts in Their Own Words.* Peoria, IL: War Room Press, 2013.

Newspapers and Periodicals

Byman, Daniel. "5 Lessons from the Death of Baghdadi." (www.brookings.edu, October 29, 2019)

Philp, Catherine. "Jackpot: The Inside Story of How the US Tracked and Killed Baghdadi." (*London Times*, November 2, 2019).

Sherlock, Ruth. "How a Talented Footballer Became the World's Most Wanted Man," (*The Telegraph*, December 27, 2014).